GOVERNANCE

A Tale of a Prophet

DANIEL DOUGLAS

First published in Australia by Aurora House
www.aurorahouse.com.au

This edition published 2024
Copyright © Daniel Douglas 2024

Cover design: Donika Mishineva (www.artofdonika.com)
Typesetting and e-book design: Amit Dey (amitdey2528@gmail.com)

The right of Daniel Douglas to be identified as Author of the Work has been
asserted in accordance with the Copyright, Designs and Patents Act 1988.

ISBN number: 978-1-922913-93-7 (Paperback)

NATIONAL
LIBRARY
OF AUSTRALIA

A catalogue record for this
book is available from the
National Library of Australia

Distributed by: Ingram Content: www.ingramcontent.com
Australia: phone +613 9765 4800 |
email lsiaustralia@ingramcontent.com
Milton Keynes UK: phone +44 (0)845 121 4567 |
email enquiries@ingramcontent.com
La Vergne, TN USA: phone +1 800 509 4156 |
email inquiry@lightningsource.com

CONTENTS

How to Read this Book   v

1. God   1

2. The Human Morality   35

3. War   53

4. The Commands   83

5. The Conversation   111

6. Guidance   178

7. The Ending   197

About the Author   201

References   203

HOW TO READ THIS BOOK

Governance has been written to provide guidance on how to enrich and improve your life. It blends the spiritual with religion to provide valuable insights to the reader on how to lead a moral and fulfilling life.

There are a few ways in which Governance can be read. If you are not comfortable using the word God, it could be changed to Creator or Source, thereby bringing in the spiritual element to the book.

However you read this book, it provides thoughtful philosophical discussion, concluding with an uplifting message in uncertain times.

1

GOD

There was a man in an open field under blue-sky clouds like the ocean waves. With a cold chill the man meditated on the idea of God. He asked the Lord for understanding. No sooner had he asked, his meditative chant and the beginning of his journey as a prophet began.

God is the sun setting. God is the moon rising with the tides. God is a baby's cry at birth, and it is the face of the dying. Some died smiling, others do not before the life leaves the body.

May you be smiling.

God is all.

All things stem from the Creator who is
the primary causation of the universe.
It is far easier to say what is not God, and the
answer is nothing.
God is all.

If there was no God, you would be a child playing with a
toy that did not exist, while not existing yourself.
It is far easier to say what is not God.
Nothing.
God is all.

God is the air you breathe, the ground you stand on,
what you see, what you cannot see.
You live and breathe God.
God is the great reality of our time. To believe in reality
is to believe in God.
To deny reality is to deny God.
God is truth, the truth is what is, and the truth is God.
Knowing truth is to know God.
God is good and good God is.

To believe in good is to believe in God.

God is love. To know love is to know God.

God is the most enlightened for he is in all things. To be enlightened is to realise you are a part of the reality of God.

God is hope. Whoever so possesses a belief in God will not despair.

God is Joy. Whoever experiences joy should know they are blessed.

God is fearless for those who fear him have nothing else to fear.

God is all knowing for without him, there is nothing left to know. If you wish for knowledge, look into the reality of God.

God is all powerful. Without him there is no power. If you wish for power, seek God.

God is the infinite, having no beginning or end, in which we experience our finite lives.

If one wishes to no longer be finite, one should accept the infinite.

God is a king for without him, there are no kingdoms.

God is a dream. He speaks and is forgotten by morning.

God is the law for he has set in place all natural laws.

God is the way for without him, there is no way. For
those who have lost their way, seek God.

God is a conqueror for all nations he shall conquer. All
conquerors look to God.

God is wisdom and the wise know God.

God is peace for those who walk with him shall
experience peace.

God is order for there is a natural order to reality.

All faces are God's faces. All eyes are God's eyes. All
hands are God's hands and all answer to him.

So, who looks into the face of God and sees an act of God
is ever present in reality.

God is the will for all wills are his; nothing is done that
He does not allow.

God is a test for this life is but a test.

God is respect for he has shown he has valued humanity.

God is ever present for he is in all things.

God is forgiveness for he alone can forgive sins.

God is the light for without him, there would be
darkness.

God is justice for the just live by the values of God.

God is holy for with him all things may be whole and
good.

God is all.

The Prophet saw black clouds like a stormy sea
overhead, and the ocean above began to empty on the
ground.

He continues to chant. The rain fell around the Prophet,
but not a drop touched him.

Even the Deceiver is a part of the reality of God. He is the
god of self.

The Deceiver is a liar for he has abandoned truth.

The Deceiver is bad for he has left no good action behind
him.

The Deceiver is hate. He hates everyone and everything,
and in the end, he even hates himself.

The Deceiver is endarkened for he cannot see past himself.

The Deceiver is despair. To follow him will end in despair.

The Deceiver is sadness for you will experience a loss.

The Deceiver is fear because you will have to fear the wrath of God.

The Deceiver is not all knowing for he is an individual.

The Deceiver is powerless for he has rejected God.

The Deceiver is finite. He will have his time.

If one wishes to be finite, accept the Deceiver for you will have your time.

The Deceiver will call himself a king, but he is a dictator.

The Deceiver is a nightmare for he will be amongst your nightmares.

The Deceiver is an imposer as he tries to impose his own laws.

The Deceiver is the easy way, and the lost often seek it.

The Deceiver is a destroyer for he wishes to destroy all nations. Destroyers look to him.

The Deceiver is a fool, and all fools know him.

Some faces, eyes and hands will choose the Deceiver but,
in the end, they will answer to God.

The Deceiver possesses some faces, eyes and hands, and
his presence is known.

The Deceiver's will cannot operate outside God's will.

The Deceiver is a tester for he may be sent
by God to test you.

The Deceiver is disrespect for he values
no-one and nothing.

The Deceiver is fear for with him you
will have much to fear.

The Deceiver is chaos for he will cause disorder.

The Deceiver is present at one place at a time.
He is only an individual.

The Deceiver is unforgiving. He hates everyone.

The Deceiver is unjust for he brings warped morality
based on devalues.

The Deceiver was the light bearer of God but now he
brings darkness.

The Deceiver is unholy for with him nothing can be
whole and good.

The Deceiver is an individual.

God is all.

The eyes of the Prophet turn to the future. The emptying of the sky ceased upon the earth, and the cold chill of the breeze numbed the skin. The chant continued.

A child is but a gift from God.

To hold a child in your hands is to hold the future.

Whatever you offer to God, he will give you better.

Offer a child to truth, and they will be better for it.

Offer the child to many good actions, and they will be better.

Show a child love, and they will be better.

Teach a child they are a part of many good things outside of themselves, and they will be better for it.

Should you give a person to God, they will become a better person. Should you give a nation to God, it will become a greater nation. If you give up your armies to God, you will win many victories.

The wise offer everything to God.

If a man wrongs God, he shall answer to God. If a man wrongs man, he shall answer to man. If a man wrongs both man and God, pity him. He shall answer to both.

For a man to punish man for wronging God is to blaspheme against himself, to act as if he is God. There is no need to punish man for wronging God for God will hold him to account.

The mind of the Prophet was drawn to the idea of the wicked and evil.

An individual who does not point to the values of God in the actions is not fit to rule, for all things that they take part in will not be great or will be lesser due to them.

The individual who stands in the place of God, who points to themselves, is an example of what not to become for he will both wrong man and God.

For whomsoever wrongs many to the point of ill health and death or stands in the place of God, it would have been better if they had never been born or were ground to ash, the ash to be scattered to the four corners of the earth, into the sea to the north, south, east and west, so their followers who search for the body will be as numerous as grains of sand on the beach.

So, the wicked may never exalt the evil.

To be given a wicked end,

They will become a symbol of what not to become.

But the Good have not found God and must suffer

needlessly.

They have not defined their morality and will suffer in

the reality that is God.

All is God.

Always point to the values of God and to God, for when

mankind points to itself, wickedness follows, and the

god of self reigns.

For he who loves himself individually only loves a part of

himself, for man is not just a self.

Man is part of the reality of God.

For when man loves himself, just himself, his god will

allow anything for that self.

For what will your god allow for everyone has a god.

For many wealth and power are their god, and if that

is their highest ideal, their god will allow any means to

obtain it.

So, what will your god allow?

To the murderer, rapist and all the wicked criminals
who have shown they do not believe in the values of
God, showing they are among the disbelievers.

So, what will your god allow?

Do not set a criminal free till he has answered to
humanity and has stated a belief in values. The crime
was driven by an idea in the mind and the individual
must present a new set of ideas to replace the old,
wicked ones.

The source of all evil in the world is a set of bad ideas.

So, what will your god allow?

For it is an act of wickedness to set an individual free
who possesses the same wicked ideas.

For you will predetermine the crime to happen again.

For it is as certain as the sun goes down and the moon
rises that the criminal repeats should opportunity arise.

For the Good shall prey on the wicked, and the wicked
prey on everyone.

For the actions we make will state whether or not we
believe in a god.

So, we must ask ourselves what our god will allow

For nothing happens in God's reality that he
does not allow.

So, humanity will needlessly suffer until they find God.

For if a man is stripped of flesh and bone and his soul
moves onto its resting place, he becomes an idea in our
minds, a symbol of what not to be or a symbol
of what to be.

What is a symbol of God?

For there are many symbols in the world, and when you
die you become an idea or a symbol in someone's mind.

For the actions you make bear you title, and all good
titles are God's, making an individual a symbol of God.

For all the prophets have become symbols of God sent
with messages and commandments.

Gods will be absolute, and until man finds God, he will
suffer needlessly.

Those who are on their way to God seek peace, and all
who walk with God are at peace.

God is alive for all those who live within the values of
God and shall bear witness to the good life renewed.

For he who saves shall save all nations with the
values of God.

For all nations will fall to God in rubble or in peace.

There is but one God and one reality.

So, it is the true test of any belief that if it is any good, it
can be practised with good outcomes in reality.

All beliefs function within God's reality – the values and
laws, nothing operates outside of God.

For God is the way for without him there would be no
way, nothing.

To accept reality is to accept God. To deny reality is to
deny God.

God is all.

For the man who denies God will suffer needlessly, and
the man who accepts God shall suffer with meaning.

Without God life is meaningless, and it is within God we
find meaning.

The eyes of the Prophet were drawn to humanity's
constructs off in the distance, towers as high
as eyes can see.

To find a building, temple, place of human exploration that has abandoned the values of God so far to the point of being the direct cause of ill health and death, it would be better if it was ceased and repurposed. If the people of the following cannot change to align themselves with the values of God, it would be better for the speakers of the construct to correct their hate speech to align with the values of God.

If the construct cannot be changed, the speakers will not correct their speech, then it would be best to empty the building, knocking it down to rubble, as it would be a more pleasing sight to God and man alike. But man can only punish man for the wrongs done to man unless he wishes to blaspheme himself, causing blasphemy on blasphemy, pain on pain and needless suffering. To the speakers of hate, they should be jailed for a time to profess wrong and jailed double time for failure to profess wrong.

All temples are God's temples, all buildings are God's buildings, all constructs are God's constructs, all forms of exploration are God's, and if it does not reflect the values of God, it would be more pleasing if it where rubble. If the people of a temple claiming to house the Lord cause needless death beyond change, it would be better as rubble than to damage the true temple of the Lord.

If the people of a temple's claim to worship consciousness causes needless death beyond change, it would be better as rubble than to damage the true source of consciousness. If the people of a temple claim its followers submit peacefully to the Creator and cause needless death beyond change, it would be better as rubble because it is not what should have submitted peacefully to the Creator.

If the people of a building of science cause needless death beyond change, it would be better as rubble for it will be a failure to humanity.
If the people of a building of governing cause needless death beyond change, it would be better as rubble than

to damage the primary source of any governing power –
the Individual.

Do not perform trade with any individual outside the
values of God, for a man who abandons reason is a beast
of pleasure and pain. In good times he will prey upon
you, and in bad times he will be a victim of his own pain.
Do not perform trade with any nation outside of the
values of God for in good times, it will be a beast of prey,
and in bad times, a beast of sickness.
All trade should be done under God.

The Lord took the Prophet on a journey deep into the
mind to see what could be and what could cease to be, in
the realm of symbols a dream.
The Prophet saw.
Wealth and power reigned as its highest values, the
combined will of mankind was that of a harlot drunk
on power and wealth. All manner of perversion could
be bought and sold. For all things were bought and sold
under this corrupt will.

She was seated at the top of the gargantuan beast, riding the beast with a multitude of heads – the beast of nations – for every nation was represented.

There the back of the beast had scales, fur and four large wings, two black and two white. The heads of the beast changed in time for nations rose and fell. It was higher than any construct of man. The beast was broad, enveloping vast portions of the earth.

The beast's legs were that of heavy beasts. It stood two back feet in the sea, one foot on land, and one paw of a bear raised to the heavens. At the top of every head were written blasphemies on horns where there were meant to be stone pillars with the laws of the Lord. The blasphemies were the laws of the Lord reversed for mankind did not keep the laws of God.

There were many false prophets who did not speak of the love, kindness and peace of the Lord. They had spoken of hate, mercilessness and of never-ending war. The world reaped what was sown. The minds of the little ones were like untended soil, where wicked ideas were planted into their minds, and they grew to become merciless beasts on the land, more dangerous than a pack of wild dogs.

The world was fill with injustice for freedom could be bought for a price. The Good did not prey on the wicked, and the wicked prospered.

Mankind did not fear the Lord and lived in fear of everything. Where man previously loved the Lord, he loves only himself, and the god of self rules over the earth.

Man committed blasphemy on blasphemy towards other men standing in the place of the Lord. God gave many gifts to mankind, which father that did not father and mother could not nourish, so God took many gifts back, and the future was destroyed in the present.

Those who did find nourishment often their minds were that of untended soil. Those who did not fall into wickedness walk the earth meaninglessly for they did not find meaning in God. Man had abandoned God for wickedness, and God left man to his wicked ways for he had lost his way.

Mankind suffered needlessly without God.

The camel was not able to thread the eye of the needle. The rich man was not allowed into Paradise because the children starved while his table and belly were full. The men below did not point to the God above, and all was not as above in Paradise for the Deceiver ruled over humanity, and man bought into the values of the Deceiver, and man acted as a deceiver to his fellow man.

Man's hate grew for he had not defined love. Because he did not know love, he did not know God.

A man stood above the head of the dragon on top of the large horn, which had uprooted the first three pillars where there were meant to be golden pillars devoted to the Lord, and the man stood in the place of the Lord. The Good did nothing for they had not found God. The man said I am the ideal, but where his hand was meant to point to God, it pointed back to himself, for he was worshipped as a god among men. The image of the man was placed all through the cities. He was held above God. God laughed for God will have the first and

the last laugh with many in between. When the Lord
looked down from the heavens, he saw wicked men
point to themselves. Whenever man points to himself as
the highest ideal, wickedness will follow.
It will be as sure as the sun goes down and the moon
rises with the tides.
For when man loves only himself, he hates himself for he
has rejected the good of God.

There were many warning signs to the Good, yet they
did not act as the many temples devoted to the Lord
were torn down, and the images of the man replaced
them. The view of the man was extremist for he imposed
his will over all of mankind. The dragon was predatory,
a beast of prey in good times, for the dragon preys on the
little ones and the weak, be it young or old alike within
the construct, on the external free nations.
Freedom is there for one to choose good, and God is
good, so choose God, and the people were not able to
choose. For the temples devoted to mankind's free
beliefs are as small embassies to freedom, and when they

are torn down defiled, know this extremism is one of the warning signs to you.

Yet another warning sign is the abandonment of God where mankind points to himself as the ideal, and a man who points to himself is to wickedness, as a fly is to shit. A predatory nature to prey internally until united, then externally, the dragon has showed its head many times. It is the god of self. It can and will appear in any construct where mankind points to himself.

When the dragon turns red with the blood of innocents, humanity is empowered to act.

The beast of nations and all heads perform trade with the head of the dragon. All pillars shatter, and upon each head sprouted ten horns of blasphemy. For many peoples of many nations had abandoned the laws and values of God, and so God abandoned them to the pain and pleasure of mankind to needlessly suffer until they found God.

For all constructs that do not reflect God will turn to rubble. All will bow to God, and he will have the first and the last laugh. Mankind will be here and gone, but God will always be.

What will it take for the will of mankind to become a fine lady upon the back of the beast of nations? If the children do not starve, will the rich man enter Paradise? Father does father and mother will nourish.

To the minds of that of unkept soil if tended to by mankind to plant the idea of God into them, will not become that of a pack of untamed dogs but that of people of many great nations upon the earth. To the heads of the beast with ten horns will all nations embrace the Lord to uproot the ten horns with ten pillars of stone.

Will the head of a dragon lose its predatory nature towards the weak, free and return to being a beast head found within the nation?

Will man point to himself or will he point to God to truly love himself?

Will the prophets speak of the truth, love and peace of the Lord to fill the world with the good news of the Lord so the lands may be filled with a sustainable

peace. For it will be mankind who will reap
the goodness that it sows to the good man,
and the wicked man evil.

The beast will be a multitude of all nations. It will move
with a rapid speed upon the earth, not bound by land,
sea or sky, for the Good will have defined their morality,
preying upon the wicked.

For those who fear the Lord have nothing else to fear.

I see the will of God; it was the Good Will upon
humanity. Those who possessed it were a blessing upon
the earth. Many thank the Lord for delivering such a gift
to humanity; those who did not possess it were a curse
upon the land, and many regretted such an individual
was ever born.

The Prophet saw the will of humanity change to that
of a fine lady for mankind wished good unto itself. All
trade was performed under the values of God as the land
was filled with injustices. It was now filled with justice
and peace for all was traded under God.

No true justice can be attained without God, for
mankind will be judged.

The beast of nations was a timeless stencil for humanity
to look through to determine the state of the world.
Not all has come to be, and humanity will needlessly
suffer until it finds God.
While the beast of nations with the woman on its back
is a part of the great reality of God, do not worship the
beast, but
worship God alone.

The Prophet saw two hands of the Lord in both hands,
where individuals in the right hand he held close to him
for they were close to God, the other hand he held far
away flat open with a tilt to the darkness. In the right
hand, they had followed the commands, acting the
values of the Lord for they had acted rightly in the eyes
of the Lord, bearing many titles of the Lord for all good
titles are his. He held them close to him for they believed
in God making them the believers.
In the left hand the Lord looked with sadness for it
was the disbelievers, those who did not follow the
commands of the Lord, those who acted in the values of

the god of self, for they acted wrongly in the eyes of the Lord. They bore many bad titles for all bad titles are the god of self, the Deceiver. The Lord held them far from him for they disbelieved and where they disbelieved, they were the infidel.

The image of the upright and the crooked man entered the Prophet's mind, which he contemplated.

Beware of the individual who bears false title for they will claim to be true and speak nothing of it.

They will claim to be good and not act it out.

They will claim to be lover and enact hate upon you.

They will say we are but one and act to self-interests.

They will say I forgive you and never truly forgive.

They will say they can see the good in you and truly be despairing towards you.

They will say trust me, and their actions towards you will only breed distrust.

They will take pleasure in your pain, and there will be no joy.

Beware the bearer of false title.

A father who is not a father to you.

A mother who is not a mother to you.

A daughter who is not a daughter to you.

A son who is not a son to you.

A brother who is not a brother to you.

A sister who is not a sister to you.

A child who is not a child to you.

A leader who is not a leader.

Beware the bearer of false title, they will act outside the values of God.

Become the bearer of true title, speak the truth and be true.

Become good for the Good will meet with the Lord.

The good man who sows good seed will reap a good harvest.

A man who enacts love will receive love for man will return like with like.

For the man who acts to be a part of many things greater than himself will reap far greater than if he only acted as an individual.

For the man of hope, he will see great good in the world and act upon it. He will see God in everything for God is good.

The world will open up to the hopeful man.

To the man who acts good will build true trust

built on action.

For the man who can see value in all people

will be respected.

The man who experiences joy experiences God.

Such individuals who enact the values of God, they bear

true title.

When the flesh, blood, and bone decay, the soul moves

on to its final destination, and the individual will

become an idea in the mind of what to become.

Beware the man with the forked tongue of a deceiver for

he will speak much hate, much division.

All his words and actions will say

"I want no good for you."

For man who hates has cursed himself and others. Those

who walk the path of hate are far from God.

God is peace.

For the man with such a tongue there will be no peace

and all will turn against him. The world will be close to

him bringer of despair.

For hate is with no end but the grave, and who is to
know its true end.

It is far better if man did not hate.

For you shall do what wicked man shall not.

You shall speak of Good.

For he who speaks of love, his words speak as if to say "I
want good for you".

Man is to speak with good intent, or it would better if he
did not speak at all.

So, it is a true test of an individual how one treats the
weakest for that is their true character.

So, it is the true character of any nation in how they
treat weaker nations for that is their true character.

The one who extends the hand of kindness towards the
weakest will find good stead with the master.

There is no higher power than God.

He who completes a small task in the eyes of the Lord
may complete greater tasks.

He who finds the answers to smaller questions may
answer greater questions.

He who acts outside the values of God does
not believe in the Lord.

He who acts inside the values of God is a believer.

He who better understands himself better
understands God.

He who understands God understands himself.

For man is part of the great reality of God.

He who knows nothing of himself knows nothing of
God.

For man is not just a self.

Show man he is so interconnected with his reality it will
be as if it were his own hands, to harm others would be
seen as cutting one's own hand. Man would be less for it.

It is far harder to harm something that is a part of you.

Man sees himself as just a self, and he will do anything
to protect that self, the god of self resides in the mind of
such a man.

Man who loves only himself does not.

When man see himself as part of others, he will do
anything to protect that reality, and God resides in the
mind of such a man.

Man who loves others truly loves himself.

God gave man reason to separate him from the beasts, for without it, man is driven by pleasure and pain. It is only through higher thought man may escape the never-ending cycles.

For it will be as sure as the sun goes down and the moon rises with the tides.

All of humanity be that of the spirit, for we are all of the spirit, those of the good will and those of the god of self.

You are that of the spirit.

You are filled with the spirit of truth, filled with the will to do good, driven by love and part of the greater reality of God.

Or

You are filled with the spirit of lies, driven by the spirit to perform wickedness, the wish of no good, fuelled by torment and hate and deny being part of any greater good.

Humanity be that of the two main spirits.

That of the Deceiver and that of God.

Prey not on the weak for it will show your true
character.
Know this—we come into the world, and we leave it too
in a state of weakness.
It is in the defence of the weak we become strong.
Extend the hand of kindness to the weak, and show your
true nature of one who has found God.
With God man can change his fate for a better fate.
With God all things are possible.
If a man be a liar, he may change to be truthful and reap
a better fate.
If a man acts poorly, he may change to act rightly and
reap a better fate.
If a man is hateful, he may learn to love and achieve a far
greater fate.
If a man is endarkened, he may learn to see how he is
part of many things greater than himself and reap a
better fate.
Man can be unforgiving and learn forgiveness and meet
with a greater fate.

Man, who cannot see good in the world, may become
hopeful and see his fate change.

Man, who is disrespectful, may learn to value others and
fate be changed.

To the man of sadness, may he experience again the
feeling of joy, to experience the goodness of God and fate
be changed.

There is something that can only be described as
spiritual as a baby who has never walked, like the blind
who have not seen, like the deaf who never heard a
sound, and with God, man's fate be changed.

For all is fate determined should man not know God, he
will suffer needlessly but with God man's fate be changed.

For nothing good is achieved without God, and you live
and breathe the reality of God.

All in him has its being.

All is God.

The Prophet looked into the reality of God to see the
face of God. It was made up of many faces, and there
were many eyes, many hands, and all answer to him.

The Prophet said I have seen the face of God

and it has smiled upon me.

There was an hourglass that never emptied

in the mind of the Prophet.

It was eternal

For time was only for man and not for God.

For in God, you will have the time.

A good master is a good servant who is at service to all.

He who comes in the name of the Lord embodies the

values of God.

The servant of the Lord is in service to his values, a

servant to love, a servant to truth, indeed a servant. For

the best masters are good servants for they serve all.

He who does not embody the values cannot

be guided by God.

When the prophets speak, know the Lord speaks

through the Prophet.

When the prophets listen to the reality, God speaks to

the Prophet.

The Prophet said there have been many great ones

before me, and there will be many after me, and there

will be one, I am unfit to offer guidance.

For many are great but so few are good. The only
difference is one may point to themselves or God.
The Prophet asked the Lord what to prophesy. A voice
called to him on a high mountain, and so the Prophet
began the journey.

At the start of the journey, the Prophet turns to see.
There was an individual walking on the straight and
narrow path with a mind, heart and actions of truth,
good, love, joy, peace, respect, responsibility with all
the values of God for all good titles are God's. The
enlightened individual walks with God, and many
walked the narrow path, and it was said that "Mankind
will needlessly suffer until they found God".

God is all.

2

THE HUMAN MORALITY

There was a philosopher who studied much
literature in the hopes of ending all evils in the world.
He studied in the home library. He was disturbed
by his daughter, very much a child, who asked
what her father was doing, and so the philosopher
began to explain the human morality.
He began by saying, "I see a wise man and
he followed a star".

To teach a morality before the law is a kind act
to humanity. It is a necessary act, for the source
of all evil is a set of bad ideas.
When one understands this, it is as simple as
changing the set of ideas one possesses. Under the

right conditions, an idea will be accepted. The human morality is a set of ideas designed to predetermine a better fate for humanity, for mankind needs to become master of his fate. To change the ideas in one's head is to change the cards in one's hands. It is to load the dice to predetermine the numbers. It is possibly the greatest act of kindness to teach a morality before the law.

Natural law is the law of morality undefined.
It is undefined as all laws stem from natural law or nature, which can be seen as a construct of God.
There is a natural beauty and harshness to natural law.

For man who has not defined his morality is as a wooden ship in a stormy sea at night with no bearing, no rudder. He is lost between his feelings, instincts and environment moved by nature, not fully conscious of his final destination. He is most certainly lost.
That which is not defined will surely evade you.
The morality of natural law is mainly comprised of instinct, feelings and environment. This is the triangle pointing down of the symbol of the star, when man

is not master of these three factors, his loss certainly being moved as if fated like a ship in a storm with no bearing or rudder.

As soon as man defines these three points, he becomes aware of factors he is driven by and can become master over fate, predetermining a better outcome. When one defines their feelings, they will gain better control over them, reducing the unwanted effect. To know their correct application, the one point of feelings is broken into two steps the naming/definition and correct integration.

Instincts are the actions done without deep thought. They are often taught to individuals through a process of repetition. Others are so ingrained the origin can be seen as near primal. When one understands instincts, they can ingrain new ones and learn to control old primal instincts.

Instinct can be seen as the daily task done with little thought with which we should ask ourselves are they value adding. Are they leading us along the right path?

The environment can be seen as the environment of the room. It is social; it is also a physical environment.

The better environment promotes better outcomes. Environment can be broken into three major categories, which are yourself, others and the environment or the three points of reality, which encompass all.

This is half of the star, my dear child.

Triangle of the star pointing down: Point one: environment. Point two: instincts. Point three: feelings.

Three points of reality: yourself, others and the environment.

For all of reality can be broken down into these three points with cross over, for there is but one reality.

From the three points of reality comes the idea of the total good. The idea behind the total good is one's actions should always aim to the total good.

Total Good: Good for yourself, good for others and good for the environment.

Whatever a person values they will act to the good of it. Generally, it is centred around the individual, then out to others, and then out to environment. This is subject to being relative, a person may value others first or

environments but nevertheless we should all aim
for the total good.

The world is in a constant state of change. This is the
nature of the world, that it is subject to the Law of Moral
Relativity.

The Law of Moral Relativity: in one circumstance, something
is relatively true, and in another, it is relatively false.

This can be used to pick any argument apart, and all
arguments should be pulled apart to fully understand
ourselves as we seek moral absolutes.

"Here is the triangle that points up of the star."

The triangle of the star pointing up: the points are
moral, values and reason.

Moral is the little hidden rules found in all stories.

Humanity's morality is encased in story; the moral
is the refined hidden meaning displayed in story.

Moral is a rule for better survival that can be
practised to the total good.

The point with moral is made up of two parts: moral
and immoral.
Immoral is a rule also found in a story. It is a rule
that is not good. Just like a moral, an immoral
is hidden in a story also.

Immoral is a rule that is not for better survival,
that cannot be practised to the total good.

Immoral displays the darker nature of humanity driven
by desires. Man needs to define his morality for if he
does not, his desires will rule over him, and he will be a
beast of pleasure and pain.
Fear not defining the immoral. It is as important to
understand as the moral. To deny a person is capable of
evil does not make them not capable of it.
Texts from all cultures should be read to understand
the human morality. It is to be as diverse as there is
literature.

The second point of the triangle is values are valuable like an
item. There are also higher values, which are ingrained into

culture like truth, goodness, love and enlightenment. A basic value can be seen as something that an individual values individually, like a certain type of art that attracts them. A higher value adds value to the individual when practised; they also add value to groups of individuals right up to humanity. These are the conditions of a higher value. A system of values will be required for humanity to progress.

A value will become toxic if only practised by one part of the whole. Humanity is made up of many parts called the individuals. If you practice a want for good and another individual responds with hate, the relationship, the value, may be seen as toxic. Know this – once an individual has defined their values, they will be able to see who practices them and who does not, making it clear who to avoid and what to attain.

The values that are also adjoined to devalue; a higher devalue is anything that can detract from individual or individuals right up to the scale of humanity. The devalue can be seen also as an individual thing, like a bad practice, like heavy alcoholism, or an item like waste. As there is a higher set of values, so it is there

is a higher set of devalue. They are lies, bad, hate,
endarkenment and so on.

The third part are enhancement traits. They can be seen
as traits that bring out an individual's true character.
They are lust, knowledge, power and so on. By their
function they can be seen as both devalue and value.
An individual may use power for good or for great evil.
A person may use lust in a good relationship, or they
may use it in a bad one. Knowledge can be used to create
many good things, or it can be made to create items of
great wickedness.

The third point of the triangle pointing up is reason.
Reason is the thought process with which one deduces
a certain outcome. If it were mathematical, it would
be the calculating processes, displaying how one has
come upon the answer. Reason is a higher process
of thought where one can project an idea forward in
the mind. It manifests in speech, words, sentences,
paragraphs, books and libraries.

The reason that moral and value triangulate upon each other is where you find a moral, you will find something you value. When you find something of value, you will have a reason to value it. Where you find one of these, the other two will be. The articulation of human morality is the necessary process to understand, otherwise the constant cycles of evil in the world will needlessly repeat.

There are many sets of ideas present in the world. Not all are displayed as inclusive due to the process of in-dividualisation. This process is articulated in story as dark characters. As the Deceiver fails to see himself as a part of the great reality of God, so it is when a human gains a title that causes them to reject humanity as a whole, then the in-dividualisation process has begun.

In-dividualisation is seen as the opposite of enlightenment. While enlightenment is seen as the realisation you are part of something inherently good and to act to the good of it, so, in-dividualisation at the lowest level is where the individual only acts to

the self-interest, separate from the rest of humanity.
Advance in-dividualisation is a grouping of individuals
driven by a set of ideas for a common cause who
have come together in a somewhat enlightened way.
Ultimately it is endarkenment because it fails to
acknowledge the greater part of humanity as a whole
and is in-dividualisation.

It is a failure to see the humanity in others.
The segregation of humanity is a great evil to define. It
is the necessary feat to overcome the evil in the world.
This process is in a constant state of repetition, constant
cycle, it will require conscious beings to predetermine a
different outcome for humanity.

The human morality is a basic set of principles or ideas,
while many constructs of human thought can be seen as
non-inclusive. The human morality is an enlightening
process where one may look into all culture to derive
their morality. The abandonment of culture is a crime,
and culture is valuable while it adds value to humanity.

The linking of value to God is an essential process for those who practice a set of values present a belief in God, a belief in something greater than themselves. It can be seen as the old ushering in the new.

Enlightenment is the only path forward for humanity to avoid needless suffering. It will not be possible without looking into the culture, the history of human articulation of the great human morality. The abandonment of God can be seen as the abandonment of values. When a people perform such a task, they very often fail to create a sufficient set of values, and the abandonment of values is the precursor to any culture's collapse.

The process of defining higher values is to define them to describe the action, while to be hopeful is to see the good in someone or something and be able to act upon it. The task is to describe a universal definition, to describe every hopeful action or every action of the value. While it is the duty of the intellectual to provide such basic constructs of thought, all people should be encouraged to define their morality, the process is dynamic.

This will lead to individuals discovering new values and the full articulation of them. Freedom is a greatly misunderstood idea. Freedom is an individual ability to choose good, which is often confused as doing what you want. The devalue to freedom is extremism, a more modern devalue which plagues humanity. It is to impose your will over another's freedom or their ability to choose good for themselves.

The linking of higher values can be assigned to God, and the process is easy for all things stem from God the Creator. To believe in God, you practice the values of God. The devalue can be assigned to the god of self, the Deceiver, which shows those who practice extremism display a nonbelief in God through their actions. This process can be repeated with any value to devalue, to construct a framework of thought.

One of the greatest evils in the world is the in-dividualisation process where individuals cannot see past themselves to the greater humanity. They are part of the failure to see the humanity in others. Humanity is mentally undergoing the constant progression of ideas. What ideas will progress? Will ideas of reason of higher thought or will lower ideas whose bedrock are desires, be thought of as unreasonable? Will humanity progress mentally or will we give in to desire above reason and become no better than animals?

To suggest an idea is to manipulate you when done to coerce another's freedom. When someone fully reasons with another allowing their freedom, it is guidance. Reason is to be taught from a young age, for the child who cannot be reasoned with will be taught by pleasure and pain, truly brutal teachers. So it is, an individual who does not possess this higher thought pain and pleasure will master in a sense.

Reason is the philosophical.

Reason can be broken into two parts: good thought logic, where one thinks towards good outcomes for humanity, and poor thought of the radical, where one works towards poor outcomes for individual gain.

Higher values have been assigned to God; this is critical for many of the world's greatest crimes happen for the reason mankind fails to see – we are all connected.

Now we all share the same set of values. Higher values have been assigned to God. They are also the values of a human being for it is said we are made in the image and likeness of God.

Spirituality can be seen as the old; the old should usher in the new. The human morality is a set of ideas.

It can be seen as a cup of coffee. If placed on the wooden table, it will mark it. The human morality is a coaster to place under the beverage.

The idea of a morality is a human safeguard that can be taught to protect the world from basic evils caused by basic ideas of wickedness early in one's life. Spirituality is not the only construct of humanity that requires safeguard of thought – science, government, in fact, all constructs of humanity require it. A basic set of values is the only way humanity will escape the constant recurring cycles of evils upon the world.

Here is the six-pointed star complete shining bright.

Morals, values, reason, instincts, feeling and
environment.

In the centre of the six-pointed star, you will find

meaning or meaningless depending on one's actions

that will show what one finds meaningful,

which will lead you to God.

As morality is encased in story, so it is we will display

our morality in the story of our own lives.

The ultimate idea behind the wise man following

the star is to find God, and we all have a God.

The wise man offers a gift to God, but to know this

God is the greatest gift of all.

Whatever you give to God, he will give you better.

The wise men offer gold, frankincense and myrrh,

and in return, we received the Saviour.

The Narrator:

The Philosopher was surprised his daughter

was able to sit through his lengthy talk,

and she smiled and left.

He contemplated the solution to the evil in
the world. Ultimately, he discovered evil resides
in the mind as an idea.

The Philosopher, climbing a high bookshelf
to great heights, slipped and fell; books struck him.
The man was unconscious and ventured into the realm
of dreams. In the darkness, he sees the light;
there was the voice of the Lord.
"I am the Lord. I have given man higher functional
thought called reason, and yet I see the minds of the
children starve. Those who do not starve wander the
earth meaninglessly for they have no reason to have faith
in me for no man speaks of the wisdom of God. Man
cannot live on bread alone. I see many starve. To you,
man of reason, I give the key to unlock all the minds in
the world. I gift to you the gift of sharp words. So, man
may live by the word of God, you feed the many minds of
the children and change the world in a generation.
You will lay the foundation for many great governing
powers, for you did not let the children starve.

For this I will bestow many gifts on you,

and you will see the good life renew.

Seeker of truth, you have found truth in me for

I am the truth. Many seek truth and falter. The way

is not easy for I am the way; without me there is

no way. You shall fight a never-ending battle with

yourself for man is not just a self but part of humanity, a

part of the great reality of me. Your battle

shall not be bloody but one of true kindness

for with you, a nation will be conquered whole.

Know this, no man can be wise without me, for I am

wisdom. Without me there is nothing to know.

I am wisdom, and the wise know me.

To you, man of wisdom, I will allow you

to define good, the key to unlock all the doors

of morality. You shall plant the seed in the minds

of the little ones, a great fruitful thought will spring

forth. With me, you shall change the world.

Evils of thought will be destroyed. Mankind will stop

reaping wickedness for they will not sow wickedness

but the goodness of me.

To you, wise man, you shall conquer the minds
of the world so long as you remember who I am.
With me, man will be wise, and without me,
man is a fool.
So be wise and know I am with you.

The Philosopher awoke on the floor to find the entire
book section of spirituality had struck him.
He lifts his body from the floor to know God had spoken
to him in a dream.
Even though the man had a spiritual experience
and was deeply religious, his intellect would not
allow him to give into faith, and the spiritual return
to become nothing more than stories on a page.

He began his journey, the great race between
the philosophers to define the human morality.

God is all.

3

WAR

Word of the Great One, the Prophet of the great
reality of God, had filled the land, and the world
knew of him. There was a time where war forever
ravaged the land, the Prophet entered halfway
of his time on earth on his way to the high mountain.
Above the confines of a military camp standing
on the hill, he observed one of the many tents,
a sea of green upon the land like coral green,
they blended into the surrounds.
He was sent for by the great General, who asked
the Prophet how to conquer the world.
The Prophet said Ask God, bless the man,
and he began to chant.

In war, you shall, whenever possible, extend
the hand of kindness; whenever not possible,
you shall be merciless.
For in war, men become monsters and monsters
become men.
Men should remain men and prey upon the monsters.
For the Good shall prey upon the Wicked but never
upon the Good lest they become wicked. This is
the law of the Good.
You shall conquer with the tongue of a sword first and
second the military might of the second sword.
A small scroll manifested in the mind of the General.

The Law of Two Swords:

1. Through use of the first sword, you are to
develop the law of morality upon the land using a
system of values by which you can heal any people
of any nation using the values of God. The first
sword is that of the tongue – it is reason, logic,
spirituality, morality, the law, and it is the duty of
all intellectuals to wield. It can be seen as the hand

of kindness required to conquer the human whole, mind, body and soul.

For a nation filled with injustice you shall bring justice. Without the law, the people will be an untamed animal towards you. With the law, you will deal with a human being for the law brings stability and order. The law should be developed from the people nation that you wish to conquer; they shall take part in the development of the law and shall conquer themselves for the world is conquered by humanity. Mankind need only act rightly, and the world will be conquered for all for God will conquer all nations.

2. The second sword is superior military might. It is to be merciless to cut down any combatant until he surrenders to you. When he has surrendered to you, it will be time to wield the first sword. You shall aim to have total superiority so the wicked will have no place to hide. This is to be practised by the Good for they shall prey upon the wicked. For the effective use of this sword, you may receive many surrenders, and for use of the laws of the Good, you shall be seen as the just.

The words the General used to believe in were altered
and he spoke:

While it may be necessary to be feared, it is far greater to
be loved than feared if you cannot be both.

For if a people fear you, they will only obey you when
you are powerful, while if you are loved, they will obey
the law even in times of peace.

Do not estate extremist laws upon mankind for God has
given every individual the free will.

What wicked men shall do with bodies of dead
combatants, you shall not.

You shall commit lawful kills under the laws of the
Good, while wicked men commit murder.

You shall not leave bodies to rot in the battlefield.

You should see them buried and a prayer of
the people's beliefs should be said over the body.

For the wicked man will commit unlawful killing,
and he will leave bodies to rot in the battlefield
creating a symbol of hate between you, while you
will give good closure creating a peace symbol
between you. The good man will struggle to fight

your army for you will show yourself to be
just in the law and in your fight.

The evil man's body is highly prized, do not let the evil
man's body be exalted. Capture and cremate the body
and spread it so the wickedness of the man will not be
exalted, for if man sows a wicked symbol, he will reap
wickedness. You will remove power from the evil as
he has prey upon the powerless, and he will become a
symbol in the minds of what not to become.
It is a show of military superiority to lift a body. Where
the murderer will hide the body and not allow closure,
you shall give good closure.
Wherever possible, you should create a peace symbol
between you and your foe, to not do so will feed hate
between you, leading to a never-ending war.
A symbol can be physical but, in the end, it is an idea in
the mind.
For man is flesh, blood, bone, a soul and a set of ideas.
For where hate is in the mind, pity should be for it is
easy to possess a wicked set of ideas.

If you only defeat flesh, blood, bone and send the soul on, a man is not a conqueror if he fails to correct the faulty set of ideas.

Do not impose extremist ideas upon a people, allow them freedom to choose good.

This is the intended purpose of freedom
to choose good.

From this idea of culture, you are to assist in the construct of the law by which you shall conquer first.

The Law requires reasoning, which is the logical thought, the articulation where the law was drawn from within the culture. The intended purpose is to understand and without this an individual will not fully understand or embrace the law.

A people submit to the law for two fundamental reasons: it is good for the individual, and it allows for greater freedoms that would not be possible if a people where to act individually. The laws create greater freedom and maintain freedoms. This is how the law produces order.

You shall conquer with the law first and
then the sword.

Without the construct of the law, you will defeat flesh, blood and bone but fail to conquer a people for you will not have presented a new set of ideas.

Man is flesh, blood, bone, soul and a set of ideas. Capture combatants and try them under the law of the people, so it is not seen as a foreign body. In doing so, it is far harder to hate yourself.

The law's primary purpose is to bring order to a people, and its focus should be just punishment. Focus on the criminal's reinsertion into a people, by which the people should undertake constructive action.

Just as they were deconstructive, they will now be constructive.

Do not set a man free until he presents a new set of ideas, for it is a certain pattern that gives the same circumstance, and he will reoffend.

The true battle is not with flesh, blood and bone; it is with ideas.

If you kill a people's combatants and fail to correct a people's set of ideas, be prepared for more combatants to emerge.

If you take refugees into your nation and see the set of
ideas corrected, allow them to build temples in your
nation. You will build a peace symbol between you, and
the just will struggle to lift arms against you.

For all paths of peace will lead to God for God is peace.

All those who seek peace, seek God, and those who have
found God are at peace.

If a criminal is to be put to death, do not hang the body
in public places. You will reap what you sow – you will
sow fear and hate within the mind of a people and you
will not have peace.

If you do not have peace, you do not have God.

No nation will wish to perform trade with you for you
will have acted outside the values of God.

All skilled labourers and businessmen will fear you
and flee.

You will have committed a wicked act upon yourself.

To continue a path of hate is to abandon God. It is to
dig your own grave and stand in it. When man is in this
position, he can stare into the grave for all paths of hate
lead to death.

Man should dig a grave metaphorically that will never house his body. To see the fear and hate, bury the monster in an empty grave, so a man may emerge. To the criminal sentenced to death, send them away to their death in a peaceful fashion. Bury the body, have someone say a silent prayer for God knows an individual's destination. You will have said the hate ends here.

Man will return like with like until he becomes conscious of better. He will return

Lie for lie

Bad for bad

Hate for hate

Despair for despair

Death for Death

To a seemingly never-ending cycle to be as certain as the sun goes down the moon rises with the tides. Whenever man can, return like for better:

Lie for truth

Bad for good

Hate for love

Despair for hope

Death for life.

Man is limited in comparison to the infinite nature of

God, so man has to accepts these limits.

Limits of Good are when one's actions are so wicked that

to not act is in itself an act of wickedness.

This is one of the great realities of war. Where one is

merciless, he cannot say his actions are good towards

the other combatants. The wicked have acted wickedly,

and the Good must prey upon the wicked for good

cannot prey on the Good lest they become wicked.

A destroyer destroys flesh, blood and bone; a conqueror

wins a people whole.

If the law fails the individuals of action, the realisation

that their efforts have only bought time for the next

wave of combatants to come of age.

Genocide and annihilation be a truly wicked act for the

Good will bear down upon you, and you will become fair

game. Such acts become powerful symbols of hate and

fear in the mind, and man will return like with like until

he decides to return like with better.

If you defeat all combatants, re-engrain the values of
God in all constructs.

God is an idea; the world shall be conquered again
and again.

By an idea and the idea is God
All is God.

There were two individuals who entered the mind of the
General – one who seeks power for themselves and one
who instilled power in others.

You shall not be an authoritarian but an authority
over the people.

For an authoritarian imposes his will over mankind's
free will to choose Good. Be an authority who allows
for man to choose with his freedom and only acts out
of necessity when man abuses his power to choose
wickedness.

For God is an authority, not an authoritarian,
for he has allowed free will.

Being an authority for all constructs should reflect God.

If it does not, it would be better if it was rubble.

Authoritarian and extremism are one; one is the other.
It is to impose over another's freedom. Freedom is there
to choose good.

To build a governing power, you are to destroy the
authoritarian while nurturing the authority, for
any true governing powers are made up of a mass of
authority called individuals.

If God would only whisper into the mind of humanity
"the world is conquered", would the world not change?
Hold the knife to your own throat, and you will realise
one can act as both.

The difference would seem to be the set of ideas one has
accepted in the mind.

Estate many authorities, when your authority no
longer resides in a place know it is governed by many
authorities. This is what it is to be a conqueror.

Be an Authority.

You shall Fight a Holy War.

A war is with no end but destruction.

No war within itself can be call Holy.

The war that ends with peace is a Holy War.

All war should be fought with peace in sight.

Holy War: A war fought for peace and to peace.

If you fight a war with no visible peace in sight, you fight
without God, for God is peace.

If you do not seek peace, you do not seek God.

Holy means to be set apart, whole and good.

The only Good War to be fought is a war to peace,
without it there is only mutual destruction.

When you defeat a people to walk into a city and see
the image of the man who points to himself, destroy the
image of the man.

Burn it in many fire drums.

For the man has become a symbol of great evil, to stand
in the place of the Lord.

For a man who points to himself is to wickedness as a
fly is to shit.

If you come to a temple of extremism devoted to the
man, repurpose it, and if unable to repurpose, have it
knocked down. For the temple will be a beacon of the
extremism upon the land.

It is far better to knock down a false temple than to
destroy a true temple of the Lord.

If you destroy the temple adored to the man, have
the people build a temple devoted to freedom, for the
construct of the new temple will be a beacon of freedom
upon the land.

For God wishes all mankind to be free.

God is freedom.

If you see a statue devoted to evil, destroy it and
erect a new one devoted to good; if you see
an insignia devoted to evil, destroy it and have
a new one constructed.

Create Good symbols for they will aid in the good
construct of thought.

The man who thinks he is unaffected by symbols most
certainly is.

For the cause of all evil in the world is a set of ideas.

The solution to all evil is a good set of ideas.

You will conquer the world with an idea, and
the idea is God.

As a father may know the first and the last loving words,

So it is a General should know his first and last order before engaging in Holy War.

For the first order will bring death, and the last order will bring peace.

You will fight with God on your side.

This is the nature of the law of predetermination; man is to become master of his fate.

The world is deterministic in a constant cycle of patterns; man need only become aware of this factor and he will be able to predetermine outcomes.

The law of predetermination is to become aware of all factors to adjust them to predetermine outcomes through awareness.

The law of predetermination is to enact free will through the process of becoming aware of all factors to develop a new deterministic outcome.

It is to lay the dominos upright, on small flat area in a line, to knock down the first domino to know the last will fall.

The best conquerors will continue to conquer long after their death due to these new constructs that reflect God.

So, the commander shall have fought an entire war in his mind and become aware of all possible factors to ensure a victorious outcome. He will then see a people corrected, with many authorities so when the army leaves, there will be an authority over the land

To oversee the construct of the people's laws, so it is the people who conquer themselves with a new set of ideas.

To oversee the trial of ex-combatants to be tried under the people's law, for the law should be good to the people and allow for greater freedoms. If it does not, it is not the laws but a set of authoritarian rules.

The reintegration of the combatants into a governing body through constructive action.

Once a governing power is established with a new set of ideas, you will be able to draw troops to further conquer other regions of the land, the people further conquering of themselves.

The army should perform regional stabilising missions while suppling aid and construction of a governing power of the people.

Do this and you will conquer long after you are dead.

Erect many symbols, statues, insignias and temples
towards freedom and this will ingrain long into the
future the process of good thought. The people will have
formed an identity of Good.

Man is flesh, blood, bone, soul and a set of ideas.

He who defeats the enemy with the law is a conqueror,
and he who defeats flesh and blood without the law is a
human butcher.

Once you have instated a free nation under the values of
God, perform trade under the values of God.

Let the rich man be rich and let the children not starve
for we will be all rich.

For all nations will be free nations under God.

Let a conquered nation join the free nations and let all
nations be free, and it will spread like wildfire.

If only man would conquer himself. Man has become the
most dangerous beast to himself, and he has done this
because he has abandoned God. If he does not find God,
he will needlessly kill, hold the knife to his own throat,
to dig his own grave, to load his body in cages and lower

it into the waters to drown, to execute the youth by
cutting off his head, so the young died young, and the
old will live to a rotten old age.
There is one reality and one God
All is God.

If only man made a manual to end all wars, for man is
not just a self. Let no good man wish to stand opposed to
your army out of sheer fear; let it be that you are just in
the law, show yourself to be good, so the Good will not
be able to raise arms against you.
A true army fights for the freedom of all of humanity.
If it does not, it is not an army but a rabble
of wicked men.
So, it is the Good need only prey on the wicked, the
wicked prey on everyone.

If you wish for a nation to be conquered by God without
bloodshed, you shall do what wicked men shall not.
As the wicked man whispers poisonous ideas into the
minds of people, you shall speak of the ideas of God, that

of the values. The minds will be that of well-tended soil
in which good trees and good fruit will be harvested.

The nation will conquer itself in generational time.
As there is great punishment for speaking evil into the
minds of people, there are greater rewards for speaking
the truth of much good into the minds of the people.
As it is better for the man to be weighted and drown in
the sea than to be whispering evil into the mind. The
rewards are beyond measure for those who give a good
set of ideas – a paradise on earth and a paradise after.

The Good shall meet with the Lord.

No nation that cannot deselect a leader from governing
office is not free. Under God all nations are to be free,
and knowing this, the man who denies the good of the
people has made himself the ideal. The man who points
to himself points to the finite and not to the infinite, and
his reign will be as the body, a constant state of decay, a
slow walk to the grave, and so his nation will be.

Gone are the days when one man points to God. The
time has come for humanity to point to many things far
greater than themselves.

Man is not just a self.

Whenever mankind points to its self, trouble follows.

Know this, a man who fights a Holy War, fights with
himself for man is not a self and extends deep
into the reality.

When a man knows this, he can draw all things from
such a reality. To deny reality is to deny God.

All combatants work with the reality of God, the great
battlefield the terrain, but know this true evil lay resting
in the minds of wicked men. When a man surrenders
to you, be sure to kill the wicked idea in the mind for it
may seem as if we battle with flesh, blood, bone and the
soul.

The true battle is in the minds of the individual.

So, the tactician predetermines a greater fate
for mankind.

He decides to change the ideas in man's mind.

He who conquers shall shatter ideas and
reconstruct them.

If only God would whisper in man's ear, "The world is
already conquered".

The wicked shall prey on everyone and everyone shall turn against them.

If you wish to never fight a nation, align yourself with the same values of God through the power of reason.

So, you will not be seen as a foreign body. It is far harder to chop off your own hand, while far easier to remove another's, if you no longer see good in them.

Faith is the extension of reason. It is to see good in another through the process of reason and then have belief in them that can only be called faith.

Have Faith in God

It will be said to level a city filled with innocents is an act of true evil, comparative to killing a set of wicked men.

For if the Good fail to prey on the wicked, they will commit an act of evil upon themselves.

When the Good prey on everyone, is that not wicked?

So, it is a true test of one's character how they tend to the weak and innocent.

If the Good fail to prey on the wicked, is that not an act of wickedness upon oneself?

When the Good falter, we all fail.

The world will be filled with injustice.

If the wicked men possess a different set of ideas, would they act wickedly?

He who is a true conqueror may conquer a people whole, body, soul and mind.

The source of all evil is a set of ideas.

Once defined, man will know evil but not be seduced by it for it is ugly beyond comprehension.

Let the wicked man live in fear of his own shadow.

When he is struck down for an act of evil, let the wicked not know of the origin, so it will be to hit something that does not exist.

If an evil man fights you, kill him on the battlefield, so evil men will not bargain with you for his life, do this lest he escapes and finds more men to deceive to perform wickedness against them, so evil men will know their fate.

Let the world know of his wickedness and the evil man.

Do not exalt the body and do not create a hate symbol.

It will be said the death of an evil man greatly aids in the
fertilisation of free governments.

If the man when he lived was a symbol of hate, see it
destroyed in his death for hate will lead us all to an early
grave.

If the man of supposed evil surrenders and
spares the lives of many, see him sentenced
justly under the law.

Let the Good do what the wicked shall not.

The General saw a mob drag a man before a judge far off
in the distance, where tribal laws meet modern law.

If a mob bring you one good man to be sentenced
according to social justice, social standing and
popularity,

make the man safe and send the mob away for they have
come from a point of ill intent.

If a mob brings you a man to be punished in the name of
God,

send the mob away for it is blasphemy for man
to judge man for wronging God.

Man can only judge man for wronging man, lest man
stand in the place of God.

If you are brought a man to be judged, judge him under
the law. Only judge the man's actions for when he has
wronged fellow humans.

Set fair punishment for the crime with the good of
humanity as a whole in mind.

Do not set a man free until he presents a new set of ideas
with the values of God, the values of humanity.

For wickedness was in the mind.

God is the lawgiver, for all laws are drawn from the
reality of God.

God is the law.

Do not be mistaken for the one to conquer. He will
require the law, the fundamental foundation of any
governing power.

So, to conquer is to start in the construction
of a nation.

A people without the law are just a group of people.

Do not mistake social justice for justice. Social justice
is to judge someone on social standing, popularity and
what will be socially accepted.

True justice is fair judgement of action under the law.

Fair is the treatment one would place upon themselves if
they had performed the crime.

Do not forget God is good. When sentencing one should
always think of good in relation to humanity,

for one individual is part of the whole of humanity.

Do not abandon the values of God but work
to the limits of good,

for the wicked have acted wickedly and are now preyed
upon by the law.

So, to conquer will require nation building.

How can any free nation conquer in the name of
freedom that which has not been defined? One of the
greatest errors of our time was to teach freedom as to do
what you want. Such a teaching has caused much chaos,
disorder and disunity.

For freedom is to choose good. If someone is presented with no good choices, they are not free. Should an evil man say kill yourself or kill your wife, know you are not free if they are the two only choices that lay before you.

Freedom is a fundamentally higher value when not defined, then nations wander between extremism and freedom. If you conquer in the name of freedom, let no good man stand between you and victory.

The people will freely submit to the law by which you shall conquer. First should the laws be truly just, allowing far greater freedoms through the construct of a governing power. Greater freedom, wealth, power and peace be greater through an empowered government of the people.

Fight a battle in the spirit. To fight a battle in the spirit of hate is an endless battle, so fight a battle in the spirit of a wanting of good to the limits of good. Do not bother fighting a war if it is not of the spirit of God.

Without God you shall not conquer.

The laws of humanity are the minimum standard for a functional society and the laws of God are above the laws of humanity and they are to be freely chosen for you will answer to God.

While there are many peaceful ways to end evil in the world, sometimes the only end is in the death of an evil man.

Know this, you live in a world many have fought and died for.

I have seen the outcome of every battle. The only difference between a destroyer and conqueror is one may fight without God or with him.

The General's chanting ceased.

The earth shook, knocking all to their knees, and there was a great and powerful voice. The General heard the Lord.

"I am the Lord your God. I am the great liberator.

I have given man free will. Those who choose me be free.

None be free without me for I am freedom.

You are the Good when your actions point to

the values of the on high, and you shall prey on the

wicked. When your actions do not point to

the values of the on high, you are no different

from the wicked, and wicked will rule over you.

When you do not turn to me, you cannot be great for no

man can be great without me. For I am great.

I speak with you for you are the Good, and no man can

be good without me, for I am good. So, know this, I am

with you.

Because you have shown yourself to be good, I will allow

the world to be conquered by you,

For no man may conquer without me for I am the

Conqueror.

Know this, man without me is more helpless than a

four-legged beast with bloody leg left to float in the

middle of the sea.

So, stand steadfast. Know I am.

Know your kind shall be plentiful. When you succeed, mankind succeeds. When you fail, know mankind has failed.

You fight in the name of freedom, my name. Let no good man wish to fight your armies, so the wicked and fools be left on the battlefield. Let the wicked live in fear of their own shadows for you will come for them like thieves in the night.

Man with me is a man unchained; man without me has put himself in shackles.

Know this, the world is already conquered. Man need only open his eyes and see me in all things.

For when man realises he is a part of my great reality, he will be free. Let no wall contain him, let no title limit his sight of another, let no border hold him for he will be a man unchained.

To you, man unchained, the earth is yours to conquer.

Do not lose sight of me for I am in all things.

Do not hate for I am love; know I am in the wicked, but he does not know me. For when man has failed to see me, he digs many graves to house many bodies. If man sees me in all things, there will be peace, and when man

see only himself, there will be endless wars.

To see me is to see peace for I am peace. Where you once

felt hate, feel only pity man unchained, for any man can

be a fool, only man with me can be wise.

Those who fear me have nothing left to fear. So be

fearless and conquer for I am with you.

The General was released to his own thoughts, the

words uttered from his lips, "I am a conqueror". He left

for a fighting season against the wicked.

All is God.

4

THE COMMANDS

The Prophet arrived to climb up the high mountain and
was hit by heavy wind; it knocked the Prophet to his
knees and the voice of the Lord filled him.

The wind died down and the Prophet returned
to the climb.
Tired and hungry he was fed by the word and the word
sustained him for a time.
When the Prophet reached the top of the mountain, the
Lord took him on a journey in the mind. He was taken
into a temple so large, so vast, the ceiling was so high
it was near the limits of sight, and in the limited sight,
there was a perfectly painted night sky filled with stars.
There were ten large main structural pillars spread far

apart, a day's walk apart, and around the ten there were smaller pillars too numerous to count.

The spirit of the Lord guided the Prophet on his journey through the temple of the Lord. Many had walked in such a temple on their way to Paradise; this temple was the mind. The spirit of the Lord took the Prophet to the first pillar and written on it in engraved stone.

There was a powerful voice.

1. "Thou shalt not have any other god before me."

The pillar was one of the three golden pillars devoted to God. The Prophet looked into the pillar. He was able to see all the times mankind had the Lord in mind, and there was much beauty, joy, peace and happiness. The pillar shattered and crumbled before the Prophet's eyes, and it was uprooted by a giant blood-soaked horn, which screamed with the blood of innocents. The perfect painted sky turned to hot desert sun, fire loomed around the ten horns. On each horn was written blasphemy.

The Prophet was told to look into the horn, seeing all the times mankind had turned himself into god, and where man had pointed to itself, there was much suffering, and a death toll too high to count. There was blood on the hands of the Prophet for he was part of humanity which had much blood on its hands. The blood cried for justice from the ground beneath the Prophet. For there is no true justice without God, and humanity will be judged. Many had walked this path in the temple of blasphemy on their way to damnation.

There was a foul voice of the Deceiver.

1. "Thou art a god."

The voice tempts the Prophet. Are you not the finest of all creatures? The Prophet had images before him of the greatest power, wealth, knowledge, lust; the Prophet would rule over the world. The Prophet was tempted but remembered the words of the Great One.

"What shall it profit a man, if he shall gain the whole world and lose his own soul."

The voice was banished. The Prophet saw all the needless suffering in the world and begged the spirit of the Lord.

Please Lord how can humanity avoid such suffering?
He asked and received.

The horn dropped to the depths of damnation; the
pillars returned along with the perfectly painted sky.
The Prophet looked into the pillar, there were the many
names of God. For the Good love truth and hold truth as
the highest value. There was written truth. The Prophet
looks and sees the word 'Good'. The Good lived by many
good ideals; good was the most necessary value to define.
There was written upon the pillar 'Love', for God is love,
it is the greatest of all values.

There was written 'enlightenment' for humanity, which
saw itself as a part of the reality of God. 'Hope' was
written for humanity if it saw God in all things and
was able to act upon it. All of the many names of God
brought Joy, which is to experience God.
There were many names, and mankind had not
discovered them all.

The Prophet's fear was removed, and he returned to
being fearless for he walked with God.

He walked a day's walk to the second pillar. When he arrived, there was a great and powerful voice.

2. "Thou shalt not make unto thee any graven image"

The Prophet looks into the pillar and saw when mankind worships the Lord in his entirety in his infinite nature. No sooner had the Prophet looked, the pillar shattered before his eyes.

A great red horn soaked with the blood of innocents shattered the pillar, the sky turns fiery, so dry was the Prophet that sweat dried within an instant.

There was a foul voice.

2. "Thou shalt make unto thee any graven image."

An image was made of the beast and the people worshipping, for man without God is little more than a beast.

Man made many images of God; they made GOD just a man, an individual equal to the Deceiver. There were many symbols that reduced God in his entirety. The Great Voice said "They have made me, but fictitious. Oh, they have they lost sight of me." God was made into a fiction rather than the great reality of our time. Many evils were performed for every man possessed his own brand of god and failed to see God in all things. This image had made God but a fiction.

The Prophet begged the Lord, and the Lord answered him. The horn descended to the depths of despair, and the golden pillar re-assembled. The Prophet looked into the pillar and saw humanity, though there were many characteristics in the infinite nature of God. Humanity managed to see God in all things, indeed the great reality of our time.

The Prophet continues his day journey to the next pillar. There it was beautiful and golden. There was a great voice.

3. "Thou shalt not take the name of the Lord in vain." There the Prophet saw when humanity held the name of the Lord on high, only crying to the Lord in times of absolute need. The Prophet looked into the pillar and saw all the times humanity had cried the name of the Lord when needed, and God answered them.

The Lord often doesn't answer in words, but speaks through his reality.

There was a foul voice of blasphemy.

3. "Thou shalt take the name of the Lord in vain."
No sooner had the Prophet seen this, the pillar
shattered into the rising blood-soaked horn.

Man cried out needlessly to the Lord when it was within
his power to resolve the source of his pain. Man did not
resolve the issues; the never-ending cycle continued, and
there was much needless death and suffering.

The Prophet asked how man is to resolve these issues
– the horn dropped to the depths and the golden pillar
re-assembled. He looked into the pillar for answers; his
attention is dragged away by a figure off to his right,
dark and hidden by the night. God allowed the figure to
remain hidden.

The Prophet said "Who are you?" The figure responded
"I am here nor there, I am, and I am not, I reside in the
minds of many, the Good and the wicked use me alike.
Some call me Fate, but I am more than that. With me
mankind can predetermine any outcome. Before your
time on earth is done you will see some of my work
done." With that the figure faded away into the night.

The Prophet walks a day's walk to the next pillar

There was a great voice.

4. "Remember the Sabbath day and keep it holy."

There humanity rested and meditated on the idea
of God. The higher ideals that encase the very moral
structure of the mind.

The horn of blasphemy shatters the pillar with a foul voice.

4. "Forget the Sabbath day and keep it ordinary."

Humanity failed to rest, failed to meditate on the
many ideas of God. Without these many higher ideals,
humanity become a beast of pleasure and pain.

The Prophet asked, and no sooner had he asked,
the temple of the mind returned with the perfectly
painted night sky.

There was a pillar that reached into the sky. The voice
of Wisdom, which was a fine lady, appeared among the
wisest, where there is a wisdom in compassion and said,

"Man should rest for at least one day a week. He needs
a relationship with the great reality that is for every
individual seeking God in some form or another."

No sooner had Wisdom spoken,

she disappeared behind the pillar.

The Prophet walks yet another day's walk.

There was a great voice.

5. "Honour thy father and thy mother."

The Prophet looks into the pillar and sees when parents

instil the values of God onto the future, their action

predetermines a better outcome for humanity; the children

see the value of many great old ideals felt great respect. The

actions of the future generation brought great honour to the

family. They bless the future, and they were blessed.

There was a foul voice of blasphemy.

5. "Dishonour thy father and thy mother."

Shattered pillar to rising horn.

The Prophet forced himself to look into the horn.

There the parents failed to instil the values of God

upon the future, instead the values of the Deceiver were

instilled.

The action of future generations fails to value the old

values of God. The action brought great dishonour to

mother, father and humanity as a whole. They curse
and they were cursed.

The Prophet asks the Lord and order was returned to
the temple.

The Prophet walked a day's walk.

There was a great voice.

6. "Thou shalt not kill."

The Prophet sees all the times humanity valued
life working to the limits of good. There was great
order and peace among all peoples. Humanity
conquers with reason and faith by which
one derives the law.

There was a foul voice of blasphemy. With it the horn
arose, shattering the pillar.

6. "Thou shall kill."

The Prophet saw brothers in humanity crush brothers'
heads with a rock. He saw humanity turn upon itself
when the god of self is seated in man's mind. The blood
toll was too high to count; the Prophet was left to
question the very nature of humanity as good.

There was great despair for humanity failed to see good in one another. Then the Prophet remembers the words of a great one.

"And if they incline to peace, then you should incline to it; and put your trust in God."

The Prophet asks the Lord, and order was brought back to the temple of the mind. The Prophet saw humanity was ready for peace and they were ready for God.

The Prophet walks a day.

There was a pillar that held up the night sky written upon it.

7. "Thou shalt not commit adultery."

The Prophet saw when the values of God were within the relationship, it prospered for God was there.

There was a foul voice.

7. "Thou shall commit adultery."

The horn shattered the pillar and the Prophet looks into the horn.

There the values of the Deceiver were instilled into the relationship. Where God was meant to be, the Deceiver was, for the greatest deception he ever made was when he was you. There was great lack for the relationship did not have God.

With God there is order, and order was returned to the temple of the mind.

The Prophet walked a day.

There was a great pillar and written upon it.

8. "Thou shalt not steal."

Then a man walks out from behind the pillar. He bore scars on his hands and feet. He was the good thief who stole his way into Paradise, for God so loves the rebellious should they turn to him in good time. The Prophet looks into the pillar sees all the times humanity did not steal from one another and individuals were able to obtain wealth.

No sooner had the Prophet seen this, the pillar was shattered by a blood-soaked horn which screamed.

8. "Thou shalt steal."

The good thief was replaced by a limbless individual who crawled one hand, one foot opposite from each other, with such pain and suffering in his eyes for the

individual was not a wicked one. If a family is starving a
good individual will steal to provide for themselves
and others.

God looked down on humanity with great sadness
for without God, no man be wise. This is the relative
nature of morality. While it is considered wrong to
steal, it is founded upon the idea of a society where
stealing would not be required due to plenty. For the
limbless individual, the law is meant to be dynamic,
ever-evolving with human understanding. Under the
law of God, the moral is "Thou shalt not steal". The law
is broken into two parts, the human understanding and
the law of God.

The Prophet looks at the limbless individual and saw
God. The Prophet gazes into the horn and saw all the
times man had plenty but chose to steal from his fellow
man, which caused much needless suffering, and until
man finds God, there will be much needless suffering.
The Prophet asked for order. The horn dropped to the

depths of needless pain, the pillar re-assembled with the return of the perfect night sky, and the limbless individual who stole for the needy was taken to Paradise for God is Justice.

The Prophet returns upon his journey a day's walk.

There was a great voice.

9. "Thou shalt not bear false witness against thy neighbour."

There stood the great pillar white and pure. A man stood next to the pillar; he was pure and truthful for he spoke the true nature of his neighbour, to be it of goodness or wickedness.

There was a foul voice.

9. "Thou shalt bear false witness against thy neighbour."

The man of truth was replaced with a liar who allowed the Deceiver to rule over him. He lied about his neighbour's true nature, be it wicked or good. Such a man was driven by the idea of social justice that which is socially acceptable with regards to his neighbour's standing. This twisted morality causes much needless suffering in the world.

The Prophet asked the Lord for order. All returned to order for with God, there is order.

The Prophet walks a day.

There stood the tenth pillar that seemingly held up the night sky.

There was a great voice.

10. "Thou shalt not covet."

There was a man who stood next to the pillar whose worldly possessions were few, yet the man possessed everything of value for he had God. Because the man had enough and God, he did not desire anything that was not his, and the man who has God has everything.

There was a foul voice, which then shattered the pillar to the rising horn.

10. "Thou shall covet."

There was a man who lusted after everything his neighbour had; the man gains great worldly wealth. He gained everything his neighbour had: his wife, wealth even to the point of enslaving his neighbour and his offspring. Even though the man had great worldly wealth, he had nothing for he did not have God.

The Prophet asks the Lord for order to return to the temple of the mind, the horn dropped to the depths of damning lust, the pillar reconstructed with the perfect night sky.

The Prophet was guided by the spirit of the Lord to the centre of the temple of the mind. There was a throne empty, and a snake that morphed into a man. The Deceiver said, "Sit on the throne". He spoke with a forked tongue for he brings division. In the Deceiver's right hand, he held the forbidden fruit for he tempts man with many pleasurable ideas. In his left hand, he held a whip for he brought much pain. Upon his head were two horns on which was written blasphemy, on one "Do unto others that which you would never do unto self", and on the other horn "Hate others as you will learn to hate yourself". The Prophet pauses and the Lord's voice said, "Go sit on the throne".

The Prophet thought he sat on the throne, but the greatest deception the Deceiver ever made was, he was you.

The Prophet was taken on a journey. His rule was that of the body in a constant state of decay. He was man who had left God and put himself in chains. No amount of pain and pleasure could cure his hunger. He ruled over all at their expense. He caused suffering to others and became his own suffering. His life became the slow trudge to the grave. Held by chains on the throne, his rotting turned to dust, for man is little more than dust. With God there is light, but there was darkness.

The Prophet awoke in front of the throne. To his surprise, there stood a King, a man passed the age of completion. He had scars on his head, hands and feet, was dressed in white and holding a book in his right hand for he was the lawgiver. In his left hand he held the entire world for he possesses the knowledge of how to rule the entire world. Upon his head was a crown of pain and mockery. The King was the embodiment of God. He said, "I have come with a sword".

This is how all conquerors will come with the law and the sword.

The Prophet was told to sit on the throne, and he paused and ask why. The King said, "I have given humanity dominion over the earth". Indeed, God has elevated man to rule, and he is only dethroned by the Deceiver when man acts to the values of the Deceiver.

The rule of the Prophet improves with age, his wisdom grew as his relationship with reality lengthened. This rule was not at the expense of others, but a profit to all. His life was filled with many joys. His life was a long stride into eternity, a walk into the night sky. The Prophet was man unchained; the world was his to conquer. The King above said to the King below, "Hold out your right hand", and he placed the book filled with the law. It was dynamic for the law was made up of two parts, the human understanding and the laws of God. While the laws remain the same, the human understanding especially in regards to punishment is dynamic.

The King above said to the King below, "Hold out your left hand". There wandered in a man who had smashed his brother-in-humanity's head with a rock. He places a rock soaked with the blood of innocents; the rock was not a gift from God but a gift from man who kills his brother in humanity. The left hand with the rock struck the King below three times. In the darkness of a dream within a dream, the spirit of predetermination came, the jester – the joker was an integrated character, with bells on his hat, one eye of love and kindness, the other of pure lust. In his right hand was a golden domino and in his left a deck of cards. Every man possesses a different hand. He spoke to the King below "You are not just a self. You are the embodiment of humanity as a whole, and humanity would seemingly be beating its own head bloody. Some call me Fate, but I am more than that. Humanity faces needless suffering, or you can predetermine a better outcome with God. For with God, man's fate be changed."

The side of the jester's face turned to the eye of lust. "The evil use me. I am, and I am not. They lust for everything their neighbour has. They stand opposed to freedom that God above has given. They lust not only after the flesh and power but of bloodshed also. Evil will constantly evolve with time, evil man forever looks for an enemy."

The face turned to the side of the loving eye of kindness. "When the Good are aware of the nature of God, the Good use me also. They come from a point of vision, a wanting of good for humanity. They predetermine evil men do not rise to the heights of power. They possess the goodwill bestowing the values of God to the generations after them, and the world will be forever changed."

The jester spoke in riddles. "To the good man I can answer almost any question but the wicked are fair game, so ask me a question if you are game." He spoke of many great things with much dark humour and charm, of the generals who will conquer the world, the intellectuals who will define a morality, and of humanity finding God

The Prophet asked many questions. The jester spoke of the alignment of the world's symbols for a more peaceful outcome. He said "Do not underestimate the magic of words for there is nothing more certain than the word of God". He spoke words that seemed almost magical. "Until humanity decides to choose true freedom, there will be disorder in the world. Where there is freedom there will be order."

He said, "Man should be glad his words are not as powerful as God's, for man often fails to talk wisely. Often his words are fill with horrors. Do not underestimate the power of a kind word".

With sleight of hand, the jester places a hand of aces in the king's pocket with a golden domino.

Just as the Prophet thought the presentation was over, the jester pulled out two puppets on strings. One was an endarkened figure, whose strings linked to a hand blacker than black so that one could just perceive the outline of the left hand. Attached to the right hand with a white glove, strings led down to a figure in a crown.

The jester said, "You should know the difference between a king and a dictator. One serves under God and the other is deceived.

Our time has come to an end for now."

Prophet felt his consciousness drift from the jester.

The image of the smirking jester faded in the mind of the Prophet with a cackle.

The King Below awoke to the dream on the throne, King Above on his right side, Deceiver on his left. The blood-soaked rock had turned into a sword, for mankind's weapons seemingly improve with time, the book of the law – which one will he conquer with first? The King Below had pain and pleasure on his left and reason and faith on his right.

Man resides with his God at all times. There was the outline shadow of the court jester behind one of the great pillars. It is said man is to become master of his fate.

The Prophet walks the temple of the mind, and thought was like desert rain. It ran and corroded the foundation of the pillars that held up the night sky, so the Prophet saw drains, which channelled thought along the good path, allowing the pillar to stand strong. This was the idea behind a structure of thought which bought order. This was the temple of the mind, and the Lord gave humanity governance over it.

There were many more pillars, yet undiscovered, that held the night sky. These pillars were symbols of the philosopher morals, the horn of blasphemy of the immorals. This is the nature of human morality to which all cultures will contribute. There are many who point to God from all different beliefs who know him by many names.

The Prophet contemplated the nature of blasphemy, which is to stand in the place of God to enact wickedness upon yourself or others. He walked and saw a new pillar. Written upon it:

"When man wrongs man he shall answer to man, and when man wrongs God he shall answer to God. If he wrongs both, pity him for he shall answer to both."

The Prophet sees, all the time, that the Just punished humans for wronging humanity and not God. To stand in the place of God and enact punishment is blasphemy. There was order and true justice, and judgement was left to God during and at the end of one's life, for some acts against God cause a natural punishment from the reality of God. The horn of blood-soaked blasphemy arose shattering the pillar. The voice of the deceiver was heard.

"Judge man in the place of God."

There was much suffering and innocent blood spilt.

Blasphemy on blasphemy.

The Prophet asked the Lord for order. There was order once more in the mind; the horn dropped to the depths of sadness, and the pillar's shards re-assembled.

The Prophet walks another day to find a pillar. There was a voice.

"The Good shall prey on the wicked but not on the Good lest they become wicked."

The Prophet sees the good morality was defined and clear. They prey upon the wicked, and the wicked did not prosper. No sooner did the Prophet see this, the pillar shattered and the soaked horn of blasphemy arose from beneath the ground.

The foul voice was heard.

"Prey on all alike or prey on none at all."

The Good did not know themselves; they prey upon the Good and wicked alike or they fail to prey at all. The

wicked prospered, and the Good became no different
from the wicked.

The Prophet asks the Lord for order. No sooner
had the Prophet asked then order returned
to the temple of the mind.
The Prophet walked with God, and upon this journey
he beheld an individual walking in the desert of the
mind, holding a book and scribe. The individual was
the embodiment of the intellectual world on the brink
of enlightenment. The individual danced with the
devil in the wilderness, the Deceiver, dancing between
the inescapable pleasure and pain of the world. The
individual had reasoned the higher thought, escaping
much pain while obtaining much pleasure.

In this pleasure, pain only increased for the individual
did not have faith or the extension of reason. All the
pleasure in the world could not satisfy. "Man shall not
live by bread alone, but by every word that proceedeth
out of the mouth of God" where the words of the Great

One who always pointed to God. This life alone is
meaningless without God.

The mind of the individual was that of an electrical
storm of great thought. When humanity succeeds
intellectually, evil will have no place to hide. The age of
enlightenment was over before it had even begun for
humanity failed to define it. The intellectuals failed;
many intellectuals blamed God for the evil in the world,
failing to understand evil lies with man
and evil survived.
The individual dances with the Deceiver on the brink of
understanding the never-ending cycles of the world, to
dance with the devil until one finds God, to experience
the pain in the hopes to overcome it. And humanity was
on the brink of becoming master of this fate with God.
But one thing was certain, humanity would needlessly
suffer until it found God.

The individual said, "Oh, the mind what a wonderous
thing, oh, I dream of much beauty, a daydream of a

pleasant place of escape, but my mind is not just dreams. It is full of nightmares also – too cowardly to kill myself and so I will just rattle to death ever so slowly but I love to dream".

With that, the individual wandered off into the desert of the mind. The Prophet continued a day's walk.

There was a great light, an aura around a gate to reality that appeared in front of the Prophet that released him from the dream, to exit the temple, to send him back down from the high mountain, down to the desert, to teach that of the values and laws of the Lord. He was guided by the spirit of God towards the sandy place where it was foreseen a great conversation would take place.

Released to the reality of the world, the words left the Prophet's lips. "There is no higher power than God."

All is God

5

THE CONVERSATION

The Philosopher travels the world as he tried to drag
into being the human morality. On his journey he came
upon a desert, which was a graveyard for empires. There
was always conflict upon the land. Lo and behold, he
found a man, his head of hair was cut close to the skin,
dressed as a commoner in collared shirt and dress
pants, with an untamed beard. He was stoking a fire late
afternoon, awaiting the night. He recognised the man as
the great man of God, the Prophet.

The Philosopher sits with the prophet, escaping the
cold to have the discussion on how to end all evils in the
world. The fire backed onto a cave, much like many a
man had meditated on the idea of God, and some had
even experienced revelation.

A conversation of this degree was possible should man be able to conceive such an idea where the Philosopher would say it would require great reason, and the Prophet would say such a thing requires faith.

The preconditions for the conversation were neither party would commit the intellectual crime of not letting the other speak, for if he be foolish, let him sound foolish, and if he is wise, let him sound wise. The second precondition was to not abuse freedom of speech to speak with good intent in mind, knowing that even with the best intentions, words are sharp. Too many individuals had confused freedom of speech with saying what you want.

After basic pleasantries, it began.

So, the Philosopher begins by asking "Is God not the cause of all evil in the world? Is he not the cause of all things?"

The Prophet: Yes, God is the cause of all things, but evil lies in the hearts of man. When man's heart is not full with that of God, wickedness follows. Indeed, God has allowed man free will, and so, evil lies with man and not with God.

The Philosopher: So, evil may lie with man but not all of mankind are evil. It would seem all of humanity is set apart by ideas in one's head; the wicked possess wicked ideas and the Good, good ideas. So, the cause of all evil in the world can be seen as poor thought of the radical. How can one see into the hearts of one? Is this not just a description of one's most inner thoughts? So, evil may lie with humanity, but I can hardly let God off the hook. If he is the cause of all things, is he not responsible?

The Prophet: Yes, God is most responsible. He is in all things; he is there should you look. This life is but a test for man. For man to pass the test, he must be good, but no man can be good without God. So, God has set a test for humanity, who will suffer without God and prosper with him. For without God, life is but meaningless. It is to be a newborn baby struggling to breathe upon a table with no aid. There is no joy without God.

The Philosopher: So, life is a test. You see it as a test for eternal life by God, and I see it as a test of character where you will be judged by yourself and your peers. Where is the soul? How can one even be sure it exists. So life can be seen as nothing more than a test of character, and to that point, we would seem to be in agreeance that the source of evil is around man's free will, his ability to decide and act upon a thought.

The Prophet: The soul can only be understood by faith; faith is a belief that cannot be proven. It is to see all the great wonders of the natural beautiful reality of the world, to understand there is a Creator, and there must be a soul. You are man of the world whereas I am man of God, but we share the same reality, that is, of God. For you there is just this life, but my message is that of the life after. So evil lies with mankind when they fail to see God.

The Philosopher: What even is God? You say he is in all things. He would seem to be the invisible man who hides in everything, the man pulling all the strings.

The Prophet: Man of the world, God is all, he is the great reality of our time and many values are assigned to him for he is truth, goodness, love, enlightenment. He is peace, hope and joy. You are even of God, and you do not even know it – you are man of truth; you are man of good thought; you are man who tries to understand love, and like all good men, you seek peace. You see good in the world, a man of hope and joy. We all seek joy. You are man of the world, but you are also man of God and do not even know it.

The Philosopher: Faith is such a hard thing to conceive that one should blindly conclude.

The Prophet: Faith is not a blind conclusion. It is the extension of reason, an assumption that one conceives the goodness of reality that is and says there must be, and that is what faith is and faith goes beyond reason.

Every individual works on the assumption of faith for it is impossible to say every individual is good; the assumption that someone is not imprisoned is they maintain a certain level of goodness.

So, every individual uses faith.

So, faith and reason may conquer all.

The Philosopher: And all thought, that is what resides between the ears of every human being one would hope.

So, your answer to all is God, and my answer to all is thought.

Can both answers to the question of evil be right?
Will the world require both faith and reason for the end
of all evils in the world, for the worldly man, reasons,
and for the man of God, faith?
You have faith, man of God. I have reason, the
higher function of thought as my aid.

So, the source of all evil begins as a thought in the mind
to kill, to rape, to steal and indeed all evil begins as an
idea in the mind.
To rid the world of evil is to change the ideas in the
mind, and what would one change them to?
The Prophet: You would change them to that of God.
The Philosopher: And God be your one true answer.
What is God?
The Prophet: God is everything. He is the cause of all
things; he is the spirit of God. He manifests as a person
or many individuals for every mind is a temple which
can house the Lord. He talks to many in dreams and
through the great reality that is.
The Philosopher: I see the communication through
dreams as an individual who is communicating with the

great unconscious mind. This God would seem to be the
higher self or the ideal.

The Prophet: God is most definitely the ideal. Humanity
should always point to God, and no-one be their ideal
self without God.

The Philosopher: I like the idea that every individual
possesses this capability to house greatness to house
God as you say.

The Prophet: God is love. God is the love that lays
its life down for the good of another. Many have
possessed it, and those who do, do not live to talk
about it though many may talk of them. God is love.
Without love there will be no peace, and God is peace.

The Philosopher: Yes, love, but maybe we need to
understand truth. First the truth is what is,
and without it, we have nothing.
Truth is the highest of all values I know.

The Prophet: God is truth most certainly.
Truth is what is. God is the great reality.

The Philosopher: And the opposite of truth is a lie, and
it is the highest of devalues.

Lie is what is not.

The Prophet: That is a title of the god of self that reigns in the hearts and minds of many.

The Philosopher: Second highest value is Good. Never underestimate the complexity of a word as Good.

Point one: better survival.

Point two: for better health.

Point three: for desires that do not conflict with the first two points.

The Prophet: You have forgotten man is of the spirit. What of that of higher good and that of the spirit? These can be seen as the values that you philosophers speak of. So, it should read.

Point one: that of the spirit of God, that of values

Point two: better survival

Point three: for better health

Point four: for desires that do not conflict with the first three points.

The Philosopher: That is true. That of the spirit, or as I prefer to see it, values. We send our soldiers to fight, which conflicts with survival as the highest point, and such heroes risk life and limb to uphold such values as freedom. One could say many of them have possessed godly love for they were ready to lay down their life for others.

Survival be the second highest for every individual has the right to survive should they not abuse their freedom.

The Prophet: God is good, and he wishes every man to survive, but those who turn away from that of the spirit of God seek their own death. No man be good without God.

The Philosopher: So, we are agreeing health is just an extension of survival, longevity and quality of it. What of desire? For it is said desire is love, but many have performed many vile acts including murder. They have even gone so far as to molest and call it love. So, desire, the feeling of passion and drive, can only be seen as relatively good so long as it does not conflict with the first three higher points of the definition of good.

The Prophet: God is good, and God is love, and those who come in the name of love embody the spirit of God. God is truth, God is good so to understand the truth of God and good of God before you understand the love of God.

The Philosopher: So, love is based on the truth of what is the reality of the situation, it is founded on good or the want for good for yourself and others. So, to perform an act of hate do not follow that of the actions of love, which seem to be an extension of good with the feeling of love to back it.

All loving actions follow the description of "I want good for you".

The Prophet: Yes, it is "I want God for you" driven by the spirit. Those who possess it bless themselves and others, and the earth will be filled with justice for there can be no true justice without God.

The Philosopher: Let us talk about the second highest devalue of bad. Bad must be the opposite of Good, and it must read.

Point one: that of the god of self, that of devalues

Point two: for worse survival

Point three: worse health

Point four: for desires that do not conflict with the first three points

So, to understand hate we must understand bad which is "I want no good for you" and hate would seem to be "I want no good for you" with the poisonous feeling of hate to back it.

The Prophet: Yes, hate is "I want no God for you". Those who are hateful curse themselves and others, and many wish such a person was never born. The evil man would even take God away from you if he could.

The Philosopher: So, to murder, rape and molest can be seen as action of Hate for they are of the devalue of hate. The actions make for worse survival, worse health and in all cases, undesirable for the victim. Desire cannot always be love for one can desire to perform wickedness upon another, which is wilful bad actions to yourself or others of a serious nature.

The Prophet: Those who hate are far from God for God is love. Now you understand God's truth, Gods good and God's love.

The Philosopher: Now let us talk of enlightenment. Through great education an individual may become enlightened and realise they are a part of many things that are good and far greater than themselves and act to the good of it. In this strange process, we attach ourselves to ideals that will outlive us well beyond our years.

The Prophet: I agree with the definition, but true enlightenment is the realisation you are a part of God, and even the most simple can obtain it. While many ideas will outlive you, God is infinite, so best realise you are a part of God.

The Philosopher: It seems so strange that such a simple concept will forever change the world. Now we understand enlightenment let's talk of endarkenment, which is to not realise you are part of something far greater than yourself and to not act to the good of it. Endarkenment is when individuals only work for self-interest.

The Prophet: Endarkenment is to deny God; it is to deny you are a part of his great reality. Those who deny goodness will suffer needlessly. When the world falls into dark times, know mankind has abandoned God. So, man should be wise and never point to himself in his actions but let his actions always point to God.

The Philosopher: So, we have spoken of the four highest values, truth is the highest value for without it you have nothing. Good is the most necessary value to define for it is the key to unlock all the doors of morality. Love is the greatest of all values, and enlightenment will forever change the world. We have discussed the four highest devalues. Lie is the highest of all devalues, with it you will not know the reality of a situation. Bad is the key to understanding the darker side of our morality; hate is the greatest of all vices; and endarkenment will forever drag the world into darkness.

The Philosopher: Let us talk about the value of freedom one, which is so evident it manifests around a human's conscious ability to make a choice. When someone chooses what is good for them, they are rewarded. Freedom is someone's ability to choose good. If there are no good choices, know that individual is not free, so to free a people is to assist in good choices.

The Prophet: God is freedom. Those who choose God be truly free. God is the great freedom giver; he has given man this ability to choose good. None be free without God.

The Philosopher: The opposite of freedom is extremism, which is to impose your will over another person's freedom. Extremism can be practised in any facet of human life be it political, religious or otherwise.

The Prophet: God is not an extremist. Those who are, are far from God, and the god of self reigns in the heart and mind. God wishes humanity to choose him freely.

The Philosopher: Let us speak of the abuse of power, the abuse of freedom, which is to choose bad, for the greatest misconception of our time was to think freedom is to do as you would desire.

The Prophet: Your prison is full of those who house the Deceiver. They have enacted their darkest desire upon humanity. To abuse your power is to turn away from God, and it is to point to yourself as the ideal. He resides in many high places, and when the Good are not aware of the nature of God, the wicked rule over them.

The Philosopher: Let us speak of the value justice, which is based on the idea of fair judgement of one's actions, where someone is judged not based on social justice of who they are but on their actions with which they have perform. Justice stems from logical thought, the idea of want of good for humanity as a whole, where the law is held in an absolute state by a functional society rather than a state of relativeness due to a dysfunctional society.

The Prophet: Do not set a man free until he has changed the ideas that possessed him towards wickedness. God is justice, he will judge humanity on its actions. He will be the judge on the final day.

The Philosopher: Let us speak of the opposite devalue of revenge. Revenge is to enact retribution without any logical limit. It is to seek one's own justice without the want of good for humanity as a whole, to act for one's own personal desires.

The Prophet: Revenge is a monster without limits, it is to take two eyes for an eye, to gouge them from the sockets. It is to wipe out entire families, wipe out entire groups of persons, dismember the bodies. He who seeks revenge is far from God, indeed has forsaken God, to be Godless.

The Philosopher: The value of kindness is the wilful good action upon yourself and others of a serious nature.

Then there is wickedness, which is the wilful bad action on yourself and others of a serious nature.

The Prophet: The world will be conquered by God in the end for God is kindness. He has acted kindly towards humanity often. Know this, when man abandons kindness, he abandons God. He who accepts wickedness has walked far from God, and when wicked individuals rule the world, it will be dragged into darkness.

When reason and faith succeed, the world will be conquered. Without kindness and good action, the world will never change for the better, and words without action are empty.

The Philosopher: Let us talk of wisdom and foolishness. Wisdom is knowing how to practically apply knowledge in a logical way; foolishness is to not know how to practically apply knowledge in a logical way.

The Prophet: I remember the words of a great one, and he said, "The fear of the Lord is the beginning of wisdom, and the knowledge of the holy one is understanding".

The wise fear the Lord; those who fear the Lord very often ask him for wisdom. The fool fails to ask; this is why many play the role of a fool. This very morality with which you explore seems to be revealed with the knowledge of the holy one, God.

The Philosopher: It is said knowledge without wisdom is useless because one can have all the factual information in the world and not know how to apply it. There is the value of forgiveness, which is to acknowledge wrongdoing in order to correct one's behaviour. There are two main parts forgiven and the forgiver. Forgiver who moves on from the event, and forgiven who acknowledges wrongdoing in order to correct their behaviour. Forgiveness is the best outcome the law can achieve, where one wilfully corrects their behaviour through reason and the victims are able to move forward with their lives.

The Prophet: Forgiver is to escape one's resentment that leads to hate, and those who hate are far from God. He who falls on his face asking God for forgiveness has fallen in the right place. To acknowledge wicked action is the first step to correcting it so one may house the spirit of God.

The Philosopher: The devalue of unforgiveness is the failure to acknowledge wrongdoing and unforgiver the inability to move past resentment leading to hate.

The Prophet: Those who do not seek forgiveness do not seek God. God can forgive all sins and is forgiveness.

The Philosopher: Forgiver and the forgiven do not have to go together for one can choose not to seek forgiveness or to seek it, and the victims may choose to forgive escaping hate or choose not to forgive giving into hate. One does not rely on the other; it is two individuals who make their own decisions.

It would seem he who does not seek forgiveness has already fallen into hate with no will to return from it.

Let's talk of the value of inclusiveness, where an individual brings something good and different to a group, and the group is able to incorporate. Humanity is diverse and full of cultures with differences from which we can all benefit. The opposite devalue is exclusiveness where individuals bring a good difference before the group and are excluded.

The Prophet: God is not exclusive; he has sent a test for humanity. To pass the test, one must be good, and no-one can be good without God. God is not exclusive; he has let many into Paradise with great differences, the only condition was they were good. The spirit of exclusiveness is that of the Deceiver, who fails to see good in others, fails to see God in others.

The Philosopher: There is the value of hope, which is someone's ability to see good and then to be able to act upon it. If someone can see good but is unable to act upon it, they do not have hope. The one who can act upon something but is unable to see it does not have hope.

The Prophet: Hope is someone's ability to see God in the world for God is good and then to act upon it. Hope is the rock climber climbing a sheer cliff face, his ability to see his next ledge to grip and then to have the ability to reach it. If he is unable to reach it, he does not have hope and if he is unable to see it, he does not have hope.

The wicked will try a remove hope from you for they will try to remove your grip to cause you to fall, and they will try to blind you, so you will be unable to see God in the world. God is everywhere. He who possess a belief in God shall not despair.

The Philosopher: The devalue of hope is despair, which is the opposite of hope, someone's inability to see good or to not to be able to act upon it.

The Prophet: Despair is to be on a sheer cliff face and for your grip to give out from beneath you, for you to not be able to achieve a new point of grip, to fail to perceive a new point of grip, and to fall into the abyss.

The Philosopher: The value trust is the assumption someone is good through good action; one can build trust.

The Prophet: The one who is trustworthy is the upright one. They point to God in their actions, and the actions build trust, the precursor of faith.

The Philosopher: The devalue distrust, which it the assumption someone is bad through bad action; one has built distrust.

The Prophet: The one who is not to be trusted is the crooked individual who points to themselves in their

actions; the one who points to themselves will wrong
both man and God.

The Philosopher: The value of respect is to see the value
in someone and to treat them as if they are valuable
because they are.

The Prophet: God is respect. He has valued humanity
often. He who has respect can see the good in others and
see the value of God in others.

The Philosopher: Respect is relative in the sense that not
all actions are valuable. If someone's actions are wicked,
it is impossible to see the value in them, impossible to
respect them.

There is disrespect, which is to not see the value in
someone and to treat them as if they are not valuable.

The Prophet: The Deceiver is disrespect; he only values
himself and he is seated in the throne of many minds.

The Philosopher: There is the value of life where
humanity values life to treat it with value
to preserve it. This is relative much like respect
for the actions we take will show whether or not our
lives are valuable.

The Prophet: The evil man's life is not valuable. Those who do not seek God seek their own death. Many seek good in their lives, and those who seek good, seek God. God is good.

The Philosopher: There is the devalue of death where one values death to treat life as it is not valuable.

The Prophet: The Deceiver only values his life; that individual is far from God. Human life is sacred. It is made in the image and likeness of God, and those who understand this see the face of God.

The Philosopher: There is the value of logical thought, the ideas that consider the good of humanity as a whole, the kind of thought that brings on necessary changes the world needs.

The Prophet: Those who possess such thoughts have good on their mind, and God is good.

The Philosopher: There is the devalue of the radical thought, the kind of thought that considers the good of individuals and groups of individuals but not humanity as a whole. This kind of thought brings change that is not required to poor outcome.

The Prophet: The minds of the radical, they do not house the Lord God in the throne of the mind, instead they are deceived. To be deceived and to deceive such a mind fails to consider the whole good of God's creation.

The Philosopher: The value of peace, which is the state of no conflict is where one feels at one with the world and there is the devalue war, which is a state of conflict where one does not feel one with the world. This oneness is caused by a compatible set of values which underlay and are displayed in action. The state of conflict is cause by an incompatible set of values also displayed in action.

The Prophet: All is made one whole and holy under God. God is peace; when the world accepts the reality that is God, true peace will be. There is war, which is caused when people reject God, and there are conflicts between the deceived and the Godlike.

The Philosopher: There is the relative nature to war, where people of good nature are required to commit necessary acts of violence in the defence of what is good.

The Prophet: When the Good know God, the wicked will have no place to hide.

The Philosopher: There is nothing more certain than if humanity does not mentally advance, there will continue to be wars on a large scale, the magnitude could very well be the end of humanity.

The Prophet: The body of humanity is at war with its self, striking itself in the face, gouging its eyes out, crying to God, when it need only realise what it is.

The Philosopher: This body of humanity would seem to be quite unwell, all-embodying illness in a constant state of being in conflict at war with itself. This is the enlightenment the world requires that we are all a part of this body of humanity.

The Prophet: I see in the future that humanity will fight wars in a proactive fashion, actively hunting the wicked long before they become a larger rabble who cause great evil in the world. The size of the problem will be greatly reduced when humanity knows God.

The Philosopher: The recurring cycles of evil will be reduced with a defined human morality, the thought that proceeds action.

There is the value of vision, which is someone's ability to see a good outcome in the mind. There is the devalue of blindness, the inability to see a good outcome in the mind.

The Prophet: He who has vision has seen God for God is good. It is said a blind man can have vision, while the man with the best eyesight can be blind.

The Philosopher: The value of a dream, which is the unconscious vision, and there is the devalue of a nightmare caused by unconscious blindness.

The Prophet: God speaks in dreams, and the Deceiver is amongst the nightmares.

The Philosopher: That which is unconscious may become conscious. One way to achieve this is to daydream, to drag the unconscious into consciousness, to dream the dream one day, another lives in your dreams.

There is the value of the law, which is the articulation of right and wrong action, It is dynamic, in constant evolution with human understanding. It is associated with the idea of justice. It is the writing, rather than the thought process of thinking of good in regards to the body of humanity for just treatment. So the law is the written, and justice is just treatment that comes into being through logical thought and the law. There is the devalue of social justice – it has evolved from what is socially accepted and a person's position in a society. It varies from culture to culture and often stands in the place of actual laws.

The Prophet: God has given man laws. Some are timeless; others were written for a time. The deceiver often fools individuals into social justice, but let him who has no sin cast the first stone. One should always think of good in regards to God's creation.

The Philosopher: The value of humility where someone's actions bring glory to all, and there is pride, where one's actions aim to bring glory to themselves.

The Prophet: The humble man's actions give glory to God; the crooked prideful man strives to gain credit for himself.

The Philosopher: There is the value open-minded, the kind of individuals who are open to good experiences; there is the devalue closed-minded – those who are not open to good experiences.

The Prophet: There are those whose minds are open to God, and others are closed.

The Philosopher: The value to be satisfied when one accepts that they have enough; the devalue of greed, a failure to accept when one has enough.

The Prophet: The one who is truly satisfied has God; the one who is forever greedy will never have enough for he does not have God.

The Philosopher: The value of responsibility where one accepts they are accountable for their actions, the devalue of irresponsibility where one does not think themselves accountable.

The Prophet: He who is responsible realises he will give account to God on the Day of Judgement, the irresponsible is ignorant of this reality.

The Philosopher: There is the value of appreciation to realise they have received something good, and their actions will say thank you. There is ingratitude, which is to receive something good but not to realise it; their actions will say no thank you.

The Prophet: Those who realise they have received God appreciate it greatly; those who do not realise the greatness of God will be filled with ingratitude.

The Philosopher: The value of admiration where someone has achieved, and others look upon it in a good way; the devalue of jealousy where someone achieves, and others look upon in a bad way.

The Prophet: The man of admiration can see God in others while the jealous are blinded to it by the Deceiver.

The Philosopher: The value of fairness, which is the treatment one would place upon themselves if they were good to themselves and to treat others in this way; the devalue of discrimination, which is to judge others on who they are, on what they cannot change.

The Prophet: God is indeed just and fair, the Deceiver convinces many to discriminate.

The Philosopher: Let's talk of happiness, which is simply the absence of threat, so basic that everyone's life should be filled with it; the devalue of threat, which is when someone is threatened, they can respond with any number of responses – anger, rage, fear, freeze – a society of threat is one in constant state of unease.

The Prophet: Those who fear God need fear not whatever comes next.

The Philosopher: There is the value of sanity, where someone is able to distinguish between a good choice and a bad choice; the devalue of insanity, where someone is unable to discern between a good choice and a bad choice.

The Prophet: I see a wise man in a moment of sanity invested well in business; I seen a drunkard who, in a moment of insanity, spent all he had.

The Philosopher: There is one value left, joy, to experience a good gain and to feel the feeling of joy, the devalue of sadness to experience a loss and a feeling of sadness. There is a relative nature to sadness as there is with all devalues. There are times of loss that require sadness for a time, a society of sadness is a society in a state of loss.

The Prophet: The one who experiences God experiences Joy; there is no greater feeling.

The Philosopher: There are many values, and humanity has not discovered them all yet on this journey through cultures to flesh out and bring alive morality.

The Prophet: Please explain this development of character you speak of.

The Philosopher: The development of character is a lifelong process, where one acts out their character. The development is very often not who you are, but who you wish to become – your ideal self. The ideal self varies from individual to individual. This is the beauty with freedom and creativity that it is regenerative. It brings life to the dead structures, and beauty can manifest. The development of character is not who you are. It is who you could be. It is a journey that never seems to end. Nobody ever truly reaches their ideal self. It is a mirage off in the distance; it is a dream that never fully comes into being. It will be you in a fleeting moment of glory, and then it disappears, to be little more than an idea that once resided in your mind as the life leaves you. The development of character is a journey one can embrace or reject, regardless you are on that journey. You can aim at greatness or fail to dream at all and wonder why life's potential never came to fruition. It is better to fail in effort than never to dream at all, to realise that the dream within itself is valuable, that the ideal self is a dream. When you are old, to live out old age you will hold onto that dream. This character, your character, can change the world for the better. This dream you live out may become the reality others live out.

The development of character is a lifelong journey of becoming and being.

The Philosopher: How can a person have God enter into their lives?

The Prophet: God is already in our lives. We need only recognise him. We are surrounded by God; we are drowning in God. For God to enter into anyone's life, they need only to turn away from sin, to clean up their life and aim for greatness. The second part is to ask God to come into your life – you hold the door open, and he walks in.

It is abundantly simple one has everything to gain and nothing to lose.

The Philosopher: How can God be real? This very often seems like a fiction.

The Prophet: Trying to explain God is to try to explain the unexplainable. It is to try to define the infinite. So, for God to be real, he must be the most real. To deny the existence of God is to deny the sunrise, for God is the sunrise, but he is more than that. To deny God is to deny you draw breath for the air you breathe, and yet your very existence is God, but God is more than that. To deny God is to deny your relationship with reality for God is that, but he is more than that.

So that is God, indeed most real.

The Prophet: Do you believe in a higher power? Do you believe in God?

The Philosopher: It is easy to believe in a higher power that is greater than yourself. Individually, two people working on a fence is a higher power than one person working on a fence. Most of the time, there are many higher powers, many groups and titles. The highest

power I believe in is humanity, which we should all
be taught from a young age that we are a part of.
This is the enlightenment the world needs, the great
realisation that we are a part of an interconnected
humanity, to look at others to see what is Godlike
within them.

Many individuals practice, live within a set of values,
so they enacted belief in something far greater than
themselves. These values you have assigned to God, and
I have described them in action that many live out as the
values of a human being. I believe in parts of God under
a system of values, and most people do. The question is:
can an individual handle that much truth, the supposed
infinite nature of God? As the universe grows, so
people's belief in God just becomes larger and ever more
expansive.

"What of the Great One you speak of who died on the
cross? Is he a Prophet or is he God? There is much
disagreement on the topic.

The Prophet: Well, to understand this, you must first
understand what it is to be a Prophet. When a Prophet

speaks, the Lord God speaks through the Prophet. That is the word of God. The Great One, who always pointed to God, was more than a Prophet. He had all the gifts bestowed upon him by God. He was a great teacher, who taught many; he was great healer and healed many; he was wise beyond measure. He died for many, displaying Godly love.

This is the truth that he embodied God. He was the embodiment of God on earth. No-one before him or after him has embodied the spirit of God more than he. So, he most definitely is a prophet, and he is the embodiment of God on earth.

The Philosopher: Does God accept sacrifices? What should humanity offer to God?"

The Prophet: "The Lord accepts sacrifices that which are done out of love for many will crawl to be sacrificed on his altar. Many fall into the abyss for their actions were not out of love. No-one will enter into Paradise if he is not of the spirit of God. The price of sin is death. Whose death will you accept your own or someone else's?

God sent the Great One to pay the price for humanity, to be the human sacrifice on the cross. One need only accept that death, and the price has been paid, and one only need to turn away from sin.

The Philosopher: Is it justified to sentence a person to death for breaking God's laws?

The Prophet: As you will say, that is relative. Humanity can only judge man if he wrongs man. For humanity to judge in the place of God is to blaspheme against itself. There is no greater blasphemy than he who stands in the place of God as judge.

The Philosopher: We are all seeking our own good. This is relative for we all pursue different pursuits of good. You have said God is good, and in some strange way, we must all be seeking God the ideal.

The Prophet: No-one be their ideal self without God. No-one knows when someone will eventually find God in their life, for many of the great ones wrestled with God and did not just submit. For the wicked who will not turn away from the great evils they have done and they further pursue, the price of sin is quite literally death when the Good know God.

I see many constructs of humanity that reflect the predatory nature of the Dragon, the Deceiver. What will you intellectuals do so your constructs reflect God?

The Philosopher: I dream of a day when there are only free nations upon the face of the earth. The dictatorship is a dragon lying in wait. Power corrupts all this and is why every individual should have their influence in a democratic fashion. I dream of a day when humanity rejects dictatorships and actively destroys them and replaces them with free governments.

While it is easy for power to corrupt the few at the highest levels of governing power who will benefit, it is far harder to corrupt an entire nation of well-educated individuals who do not benefit as directly as the ruling few. I live and dream this will happen within a lifetime. This is impossible if we humanity cannot understand our basic core values – if we do not understand our morality and we fail to understand what makes us Godlike.

Morality is the precursor of the law. It is encased in story. It is a mercy to teach a morality before the law. It is to fill the human mind with the right programming, the thought that comes before action to change humanity forever. This is indeed a great time to be alive, during yet another period of enlightenment. What comes after enlightenment if not the age of reason and faith?

Why is there so much needless suffering in the world? Why does God not just send someone to end the pain of humanity?

The Prophet: To blame God for all the needless suffering in the world is to scream at your own reflection. Man is not just a self but part of the great reality of God. The very person God has sent to overcome the needless suffering in the world is you. Maybe you house greatness and you have conquered your own suffering, and it is now your time to end the needless suffering for others. He who possesses true kindness houses the spirit of God.

The Lord has decreed that you would be since the beginning of time, and in that freedom, you would choose greatness or fall into wickedness. As there is great strength in kindness, there is great weakness in wickedness. The way humanity becomes strong is in the protection of the weak so they may become strong.

So, the reason there is so much needless suffering in the world is humanity has not yet overcome it.

The Philosopher: What religion are you, Prophet? What religion is the correct one to follow?

The Prophet: A true prophet is not part of a religion but a part of humanity, a part of the creation. The prophets have a direct relationship with God. Humanity divides themselves into many groups caused by the deceiver, who tempts many with pleasurable ideas but brings much pain.

The right religion is the one that brings one closer to God. Many would be closer to God if they had a direct relationship with him. Religion is not your relationship with God; no individual's life be complete without God.

A person may meet with another person under certain social conditions, rules in a set location. These conditions are not your personal relationship with the other person. Religion is the social condition, the rules and the set locations, but it is not the person with whom you have the relationship, God.

We are all fully immersed, drowning in the reality that is God. The problem is not that there are religions, it is that people have a relationship with religion over God and will needlessly suffer.

The problem is not that people have a religion, but they fail to see they are a part of the creation of humanity.

The Philosopher: That is what I would call in-dividualisation – where individuals develop a title with a certain set of ideas, which causes them to fail to see they are a part of any greater good, a part of humanity. This process is abundantly evident to see in humanity; the only means of overcoming it is to first understand it at its essence to know what is the unideal and then to define the ideal.

This is the way to orient a goal to define the ideal and the unideal, to know what is to be attained and what is to be avoided. I have seen many an individual fail to define a value at its essence, and by doing so, fail to utilise in action. This causes them not to know what to truly attain and what to avoid.

I have seen many an intellectual define a value without telling the great stories, which show the utility of the value. They fail to dream at all; the value was as bland as saying this is a stone. I think stones are good, without telling the story of the stone, that it was part of one of the great wonders of the world.

I see morality as relative, held in an absolute state by a functional society that is good. I have heard of the good thief who stole his way into Paradise. These darker traits of humanity, which I would call devalues, are that which can be assigned to the shadow – all the traits that are seen as dark and of our unideal selves, when we are not at our best. These traits can be correctly integrated; these darker traits that are often assigned to the Deceiver.

The Prophet: Yes, the good thief stole his way into Paradise. He only did so because he turned to the Lord in good time. There have been many good thieves who stole for the needy for the Good will steal if there is not a functional way to provide in a society. The good thief is not the only one who made his way to Paradise. There was the good liar, who lied to hide many good people from the wicked, and Goodness saw them and took them to Paradise. Know this, when a devalue seems like a value know this is an indication of society's gradual collapse.

The good thief and liar are just the beginning. There were the good who exacted the limits of good to defend people against the wicked, and the Lord took them into Paradise also. There were those who saw such vile actions that filled them with strong emotion to exact the law. Know this, while God is of the highest understanding, hate will put even the goodness of individuals in question. Where hate is seen as virtue, your society collapse is imminent, yet the Lord took many into Paradise.

There was the good rebel, who looked into a construct of man found no good in it, wished for no part in it, who rebelled and fought against it. The good rebel was allowed into Paradise. If the Good have to rebel against your constructs that do not reflect God, know it is a sign of your society's collapse.

The Philosopher: This is the relative nature of reality, where a devalue can be seen as the right form of action, but as you clearly state, it is a sign of gradual collapse of a society. These traits enacted in the right form are the integration of the shadow. Nevertheless, it is more desirable if society is functional, not requiring people of good nature to act outside a system of values. That is only possible while our systems, our very way of life, reflect such values.

So, God is the ideal, the Deceiver is the shadow, the unideal, and the dream is the communication with the depths of the unconscious.

The Prophet: That which does not reflect God will bow in rubble, for there are many warning signs for a construct that does not reflect God. As you said, there is a relative nature to the values of God which are held in an absolute state by a functional society that reflects God.

The Philosopher: Have you ever known someone who required God quite deeply as if their life was incomplete without God?

The Prophet: No-one's life is complete without God. I knew a man quite intimately. He was a man filled with much hate, rage and anger. The man envisions the deaths of many people on a battlefield, and in his mind, he stood on a pile of bodies. As the man's hate grew, so did the pile of bodies beneath his feet, and he passed the point of being a good individual into becoming a wicked one – the line was blurred. No amount of death would bring true happiness and joy; indeed, in deep rumination, nothing was sacred.

The man saw another man who stood on a pile of bodies. Seeing a body of a loved one beneath him, the man advances towards the man to realise it was his reflection in the waters, for hate hurts us all. The man picks up the body from beneath his feet with pain and anguish; he cries out.

Then came a fine lady, who took the body from the man along with the pain, anguish, hate, rage and anger. Lady Love came and was gone in a fleeting moment, leaving the man to stare into the waters, then he submerges himself in the water and was born again anew with God.

The man returns to the reality of the world, escaping the vision, in an open field under blue sky.

The man asked for understanding.

Narrator: The individual was none other than the Prophet himself, as he embodied humanity at its best with God. Before he had accepted God, he was lost, no better than anyone else with the fallen nature, the tendency towards a moment of hatred. Sometimes humanity has to stand on a pile of bodies to realise hatred to be truly evil.

The Prophet: Have you ever sought a thing so badly?

The Philosopher: I have been striving my entire life to understand and to define the human morality. I know it is so great and vast that every story ever told encapsulates a part of it; it is as old as cave painting or older. It motivates humanity to greatness and evil; the better morality one possesses predetermines better actions.

All cultures present a morality hidden in story and dogma. I will spend my entire life exploring the truths and deceptions of every culture, even though my effort

will only make sense of a small portion of it, to supply a
framework of thought, a lens, to look through.

In that struggle, I hope the evils in the world will end.

Humanity needs to define these many great ideals to
replace wicked thought.

How many persons is God? There is much confusion
and debate. Many say God is three persons, and many
say God is but one. So please explain.

The Prophet: To understand God is like asking how one
can understand the whole of reality for God is the great
reality of our time. God at his essence is pure spirit, the
great spirit of God. He resides in the mind of every man
and is seated on the throne of so few. The great spirit
resides in all things; he is all the power there is; he is
all there is to know. He goes by many names – he is
the great spirit that presides over all. For God is above
every man.

God is the great spirit. It is said when he is seated in the
throne room of the mind of man, his mind is on fire with
that of God. The spirit of God is above every man like a

dove but is not a dove; it is pure like the whiteness of a dove but is not a dove. The great spirit of God resides in all – mankind need only realise it.

The spirit of God is that of the good son. He is willing to suffer on his way to the father. The spirit of God resides in such an individual, for on the way to becoming a father, one must be a son first. This is the way, and without God, there would be no way. God is not just the son, while he is the spirit of God, in the words of the Great One "No-one comes to the father but through me".

When an individual becomes a father, he has the higher understanding through experience. The spirit of God resides in the father, and the father loves his children as God loves humanity. God is not just the father. God resides in the mind of every man but is seated in the throne of so few.

God is not just the father.

The spirit of God is above all. He is the way for without him, there is no way, and he is the highest understanding.

God is but one.

God is the cause of all, the great spirit, the Creator, for all things stem from the Creator, all is one with God and God is one.

So, God is one, God can be seen as three persons, and God is all.

The great spirit of God is the cause of all things, but while he is in the throne room of every individual, he is seated in so few. The person of God is that of every person of the earth for he is in all things. An act of God can be seen in every day, the face of God is ever present, and the actions of God are all over the earth. God resides in every mind but is seated in the throne of so few.

So, God is as many persons as that have inherited the earth. God can be viewed as three persons, God is all, and God is one.

As the spirit of God resides in every man, know this, no man is good in the eyes of God for God is Good.

Even though man is part of the great reality of God, do not worship man but God alone.

The Philosopher: These scriptures... how different are they from our new texts and cannot ours be divinely inspired? Has God failed to speak to mankind? Of the many good books held to be holy will more be added to the library of humanity.

The Prophet: God never stops speaking to humanity. He is here and gone; he is a cry in the night; he is the sun rising; he walks with many and sits in the throne room of so few. That of the holy books he inspires man not just to look into the reality but how to act. While the Prophet preaches how to act, these new individuals of influence are barren, lack the moral value to preach that we are no more than animals, beasts of pleasure and pain. That is what we live and learn by. It is only through faith, the extension of reason, we may hope for better.

Break a few more poor souls as you fail to preach how to act.

While we fail, God has never stop speaking to humanity. There will be many new holy texts to the end of time.

While I will be the critic to your texts, know this, man of the world, you will be a critic to mine.

How will the modern individual view the holy texts?

The Philosopher: Gone are the days when religion will be taught in an extremist fashion. The time has come for all the stories to be taught along with the morality, a system of values, so one may define their own morality to become their own true self. If there is anything free nations need to be extreme about, it is the value of freedom, not just freedom but the enlightenment idea that we are all apart of humanity. The old texts will be seen as the ideas with which humanity has progressed from where they have been recorded and we are now able to build upon by ever improving our ideals.

No more will it be that people will blindly follow old primitive thought. They will build upon it to know what humanity has come from to advance to a modern thought, the kind that is an articulated morality.

So, religion will be taught to all in a subject called human morality.

The Prophet: I can only guess that if you value freedom, you will allow people to choose to be religious of their own volition. So, believers in God may be free to do so.

The Philosopher: Yes, of course.

With your help I have been able to define the moral spectrum. There is greatness, kindness, good, bad, wickedness and evil. Let's begin with greatness, which is the polar opposite of evil. Here is the definition.

Act of greatness is of a serious nature, good health or better survival, good intent to the total good, good for yourself, good for others and good for the environment.

Greatness is what every individual should aim for within their lives, to be it in a fleeting moment of glory. Greatness is above good; it is such a mediocre word and does not really gratify truly great action. Greatness is above kindness; it requires intent that which has been thought through, played out in the mind to intended good.

The idea of greatness is the human advancement in thought. It is the cure for a disease; it is the architect designing life-changing machines to improve humanity.

Who better to define greatness within their lives if not the individual?

The Prophet: True greatness is God. Humanity should aim for God; to sin is to miss the mark, to fail to hit the mark. This is very often caused by not aiming at greatness when man aims for wickedness.

The Philosopher: That which has been defined will not evade you. Let greatness evade humanity no more. There is the good action of kindness.

Kindness: The wilful good action of a serious nature upon yourself or others.

Kindness is very often emotionally driven. It is action that one may not have become fully aware of. It does not have the same in-depth intent greatness does, so intent is what separates greatness from kindness.

The Prophet: Those who believe in God believe in kindness; at the day of judgement, you will wish for kind judgement. So be kind, so God may be kind to you.

The Philosopher: There is good. Never underestimate the complexity of such a simple word. Good is the mediocre of words, while it is the most necessary to define.

Good:

Point one: that of the spirit of God, that of values

Point two: better survival

Point three: better health

Point four: for desires that do not conflict with the first three points

The basicness of good is very often not articulated to the fullest; when humanity defines such values, a morality will become easy to teach.

The Prophet: God is good, and people who believe fill their lives with many good actions.

The Philosopher: There is bad, the most necessary to define to understand the darker nature of morality. Bad is such a mediocre word, people may say they are just having a bad day, the weather's bad, it is just so mediocre.

Bad:

Point one: that of the spirit of the god of self, that of devalues

Point two: worse survival

Point three: worse health

Point four: for desires that do not conflict with the first three points.

The Prophet: Those who are deceived, their lives are filled with many bad actions.

The Philosopher: When defined one may be able to reason with another to convince them of these poor actions.

Wickedness: The wilful bad action of a serious nature upon yourself or others.

Like kindness, wickedness is very often emotionally driven. It is not thought all the way through, lacking the intent of evil.

The Prophet: The wicked have failed to comprehend the goodness of God.

The Philosopher: There is evil, the flip side of greatness. It is to level a city filled with innocents; it is to purposely let loose a deadly virus; it is to commit genocide. Let humanity define many great evils to be avoided.

What separates it from wickedness is intent, the fact that an individual had thought the action through and wilfully performed the action.

Act of evil: is of serious nature, ill health or death, ill intent, to the total bad, bad for yourself, bad for others and bad for the environment.

Some would see evil as more intelligent than wickedness because it requires intent that which has been thought through. It is nothing more than the advancement of human stupidity, the failure to answer a complicated question correctly.

The Prophet: The Deceiver knew his actions were evil, and yet he rebelled against God.

The Philosopher: That is the moral spectrum: Greatness, Kindness, Good, Bad, Wickedness and Evil. How should one develop a belief?

The Prophet: One should explore the great reality of God to find meaning within God; let the belief be tested to find truly resilient belief. It is to have an open mind to explore within that freedom to one day stumble upon the Greatness, to stumble upon God.

The Philosopher: This forming of belief sounds much like the idea of forming an opinion, which is also a

form of belief and is also formed over time. This open
mindedness is the ability to view all aspects of an
argument, to hear both sides of a discussion, to use logic
and reason to develop one's own beliefs and opinions.

Within this logical thought, which thinks of the Good
in regards to the body of humanity, one should choose
a belief that brings value, not only to themselves but
also to the humanity that they are a part of, so freedom
of belief and opinion is not there to do whatever you
want but to choose a good belief, to choose a good point
of view.

The Prophet: Let's have faith people will choose
a good belief.

The Philosopher: When we define the un-ideal, we can
actively avoid it, attack it, and destroy it. While defining
the ideal, actively move towards it to attain it. Why do
free countries harbour intellectual terrorists, the kind
of extremists that openly attack freedom while living
privileged within a free nation? Should they not just be
sent back to their country of origin? If not, should they

serve time in a prison while undergoing education in the idea of freedom, the very core values of free nations?

The intellectual terrorists' ideas that bring terror to the free thinker, ideas that if put into practice would be harmful or fatal to the common good folk, they are freedom free-loaders, who live in a country others fought for, yet they speak ideas loudly out in the open of extremism.

The Prophet: The Good did not know God. They were not able to define true freedom.

The Philosopher: Now we have defined freedom, let us be extreme upon the idea of freedom to actively seek it and destroy the extremist ideas, which seek to impose over individual freedom. Let humanity actively wage intellectual war to liberate every country from the poisonous idea of the extremist.

How can we justify sending soldiers to fight overseas when the laws fail to eradicate extremism inside a free nation?

The Prophet: God is the law, the great lawgiver. Freedom of a God-given paradise in the next life is not for all. Let them suffer or prosper in the reality that is God, and who is to know when someone within their freedom will stumble upon God.

The Philosopher: Freedom is built into the very fabric of nature, and with this conscious ability to make a choice with education, we will all choose a good belief within our own freedom. So, for the man of faith, freedom is God-given; to a man of reason, it is built into the very nature beyond evident.

The only way to defeat extremism is to teach freedom. Extremism to defeat extremism is still extremism. It is only through freedom a victory will be achieved.

The Prophet: Let the enlightenment of humanity begin to a lasting peace and era of reason and faith.

Enlightenment is the father who is unable wilfully to harm a child. He sees the child as a part of himself, a part of the family. A father would understand this truth; the father is still able to stand as an authority figure to uphold what is right.

The Philosopher: This is the enlightenment the world needs – to see every human being as a part of humanity, to wilfully wish no harm to another, to only act as an authority, to realise that what you have done to the weakest, you have done to humanity, to perform kind acts towards humanity or crimes against it.

The Prophet: Whatever you do to the least, you have done unto God. We are all a part of this reality of God.

The Philosopher: What in your opinion is man's worst addiction?

The Prophet: The greatest of all values is love, and the worse is hate. Man has a natural craving towards it because of his fallen nature. It is past time for man to progress beyond it. Man who hates in the eyes of God is spiritually dead until he finds God again.

The Philosopher: The addiction within itself is so simple. It is anytime one wishes no good for another. It may start as something that is undesirable with no higher good intended, then it may be something that causes another bad health without survival in mind. It will be something that could be fatal, and the highest ideal a person can wrong someone is to impose over their values. To impose over the truth, to impose over their good, to impose over their love, to impose over their enlightenment and to impose over their freedom.

Hate is easy to fall into in an unconscious way. It is somewhat naturally occurring as if part of our very nature, which we must rise above, and it is only through the articulation of morality, this addiction will be overcome.

The Prophet: What of the idea of expansive imperialism?

The Philosopher: We all have a set of ideas; the idea of the expansive imperialism is an idea just like any other. Humanity becomes attached to ideas that become so personal, as if part of their very image. The only way to overcome imperialism is to replace the idea with a more desirable one. The answer is that simple and that complex.

Imperialism stands opposed to freedom; it is like a predatory dragon that wishes to consume.

The Prophet: The dragon is the Deceiver. The greatest deception he ever pulled was he was you; you enacted the role of deceiver. You are not imperialist, the kind of individual to impose over others, you are a free being an authority.

The Philosopher: It is when we change out these inferior ideals with superior ideal, we must convince, we must sell, and we must reason this higher thought. Man needs a higher ideal outside himself. It should be humanity to achieve enlightenment.

The Prophet: Humanity is a good ideal; there is no higher ideal than God.

It is easy to define physical truth. How does the philosophical mind discern the metaphysical truths?

The Philosopher: These truths are that which cannot be measured. Their worth is more than one would ever think. They are the stories that help us make sense of our reality; they are the stories of snakes, God, men and goddesses. These stories we take more seriously than we ever want to admit to ourselves. We go home to read a story, watch a drama, to tell a loved one the story of our day.

The metaphysical is story, encased within it is morality. Subconsciously we believe in these stories more than many would like to admit; subconsciously they shape us and change the way we think through exposure to them. The better the story, the better outcome it promotes.

Not all metaphysical stories are equal. Some will motivate one towards evil; some promote In-dividualisation, and others were the highest ideal for the time they were written, and now human understanding has progressed.

The Prophet: There is one truth, one God, and those who choose him be truly free.

The Philosopher: Metaphysical is just another word that could be interchanged with ideology. We all possess a set of ideas; those are our metaphysical truths we have accepted. The true worth of any ideology is that it can be practised in a way that is good for the whole body of humanity.

Know this, we all have some form of ideology. To claim otherwise is to claim not to retain thought. Gone are the days that allowed extremist ideology; humanity must rise above it, above hatred, extremism and above in-dividualisation."

The Prophet: Humanity be not deceived anymore.

The Philosopher: Who shall enter into Paradise?

The Prophet: Only those born of the spirit of God shall enter into Paradise. The spirit of God is the spirit of goodwill upon the earth, and those who possess it create Paradise on earth, and the Good shall meet with the Lord. Without this spirit, humanity is predestined to suffer needlessly until they find God.

How will you achieve greatness? How will you change the world?

The Philosopher: I will write a book with a set of ideas. It will be the first domino to fall, to set off a chain reaction that will forever change the world. I will help define human morality, the basic teaching of thought, to offer guidance to the mass of humanity. This basic teaching of thought will change every individual in an incremental way on a large scale, such a change is beyond comprehension.

The articulation of feeling, instincts, environment, values, morals and reason will assist in the control of desire, which rules over us when undefined. I have seen the world change already in my mind before it has even begun; this is the nature of the law of predetermination.

I was famous in my mind long before I ever was.

It is to see an outcome in the mind's eye, to drag the outcome into reality, to make the impossible happen. Changing the ideas in one's head is to load the dice to predetermine a better outcome.

When my time on earth is done, I will disappear to become nothing more than an idea.

In this age of superpowers, how does one understand the right action?

The Prophet: I have seen the ideal for God has allowed it. A superpower should be that of the loving mother figure. The smaller nations that surround her are childlike. The loving woman bestows the many values of God upon the childlike. They grow to be many free nations, each with individual personalities. There have been times when the loving woman fails to guide a childlike nation down the straight and narrow path. The child grew to be monster and the mother slayed child. I have seen times when children grew within the values of God. The mother fell in love with her own image, so hungry for power she picks up a screaming child by the head and devours it, feet first; such is the nature of expansion.

The era of free nations is upon us. Let all nations be free under God; let all trade be under the values of God; let the rich man be rich; let the children not starve; let us all be truly wealthy.

So, the right action is to walk the straight and narrow path known as one of the many names of God.

Freedom.

I know I will never defeat the Deceiver; it is a battle every individual will face within their own lives. So how will you defeat in-dividualisation, the great disease of thought?

The Philosopher: The antidote to this plague is individual freedom. It is the idea that every individual may pursue their own personal good, so long as it is good for the entire body of humanity. This is the cry of the existentialist philosophers. It is the dream for all, and if I dare to say it, it is something God-given that which allows humanity to be Godlike.

It is not only what allows you to choose your own
personal beliefs, it is what allows others to choose
their own personal beliefs, and it is the acceptance
that everyone is entitled to this freedom. This allows
a person to be their own true character, to walk the
journey of their own lives and not that of someone else.
The world needs individual freedom; on a large scale,
it is the freedom of every country – the idea that every
country shall be free, to allow individuals to move freely
between countries, so people of all different skills will
change the world. It is to allow blood back to circulate
through the body of humanity, to bring life to what has
been dormant.

In this vision, I have seen the world changed.

The Prophet: God has given you a great dream. May he
always smile upon you.

I wish to prophesise peace over humanity, I wish to
make a covenant between humanity to uphold the
values of God. Gone are the days when prophets
interceded between mankind and God; the time has
come for humanity to point to God.

The Philosopher: This covenant should be an agreement between all nations to respect, to see the value in every nation, to be free to protect that freedom, to lay morality at the foundation, to plant the seed of greatness. In that humanity may change, the values of God are the values of a human being that which allow us to be great, that which allow us to be Godlike. Will world leaders decide the value of a human life, to decide it is sacred? Will they turn away from In-dividualisation, turn away from needless war, will they agree to a covenant of every nation to be free?

The Prophet: The Deceiver is seated in the throne of so many minds. The question is will humanity be deceived, or will true enlightenment occur? Will this body of humanity realise it is a part of the reality that is God?

The Philosopher: This body of humanity that looks like a cluster of lights in the night sky looking down on earth, will it become enlightened? Will the world experience an enlightenment?

Narrator: The question was left unanswered; only
humanity will be able to answer it.

It was late. The words filled the night air. What a good
night to be an owl, overseeing the idealistic conversation
that went on a considerable while. Who is to know the
full depths of understanding the two men attained,
one can only wonder. The conversation ended, and the
Prophet left with the spirit of God, and there was a dark
void where the Philosopher had felt a presence; no man
is complete without God. The Prophet realised without
the higher thought of reason, many would fall into
wickedness.

True faith be unachievable without reason for faith is
the extension of it.

The Philosopher, well caffeinated as he drank enough
coffee through the day to bring on an existential crisis
by lunch time, was left to look into the night sky to
contemplate the reality of God.

All is God.

6

GUIDANCE

The Prophet was very near to the end of his journey. He had reached a point where land meets sea and sky, to stare into an endless blue.

He was unsure if God wanted him to swim to the depths of the sea or walk on into the sky.

There in the mind of the Prophet, projected on the beach, was the gargantuan beast of nations to greet him, the kind of imagination, which would make any normal person question their sanity. Yet there it was, a symbol of humanity as a collective whole.

He was not the first, nor will he be the last man to envision such beasts; the human mind is filled with such archetypical monsters.

The mind of the Prophet was deeply touched by the Philosopher who had said, "When an individual fails to fully understand an idea, they very often have a dream or a vision of it. In some strange way that is a partial understanding that is quite often turned into a symbol or story. Within that story or symbol is hidden meaning, a hidden morality".

The beast was more than that to the Prophet. It was that of the spirit of humanity in its dualistic nature with God and without him.

The Philosopher had also said, "The time has come to seek the value of all beliefs, to preserve the stories of all cultures, as not to lose them". The Prophet knew the spiritual was hidden within and knew humanity would not abandon faith.

There was the assertive aggression of the General. These individuals of such drive will most certainly conquer the world; the question was only when. This will to conquer was a universal desire found within such individuals of aggression, across cultures. The world needs such individuals to perform the task of liberating the entire world.

The smell of the sea salt enveloped the nostrils; the waves rolled in endlessly.

The Philosopher had defined guidance and coercion.

"Guidance is the actions that guide, that which allows for freedom, that which allows an individual to choose their own good.

Coercion is the actions that coerce, that which is done to not allow for freedom, that which does not allow for an individual to choose their own good."

In the modern era, it is beyond necessary to define; it is as vulnerable as the minds who came before. Humanity needs to abandon the coercion of the extremist and act as an authority with guidance.

The Prophet said, "If there is anything a man should ask for it is guidance. Those who are rightly guided are those guided by God."

This kind of internal conversation was like writing a message to humanity on the sandy beach. Yet the Prophet continued with the internal dialogue. The Philosopher was no longer with the Prophet; his way of perceiving the world had an effect on the prophetic.

The conversation felt so real as if he was
there in spirit.

The Prophet continued:

Man, who is rightly guided, is guided by truth.

Seeker and speaker of truth.

Man is guided by this great reality of God.

Man, who is misguided, has embraced lies

– bought into the great delusion.

Man, who is rightly guided is led by Good.

His life will be filled with many good actions.

He who is misguided, his action will lack the presence of
God.

He who is rightly guided is driven by love, for God so
loved the world.

Man, who is misguided, has found something to hate.

He who is rightly guided has reached enlightenment and
realises he is a part of the reality of God.

Know this, even the most simple man can become
enlightened.

He who is misguided fails to see the interconnected
nature of reality.

Even the most intelligent man can fail to become
enlightened.

He who is rightly guided has learned forgiveness,
for he who can forgive has escaped the curse
of hatred.

He who has not forgiven slowly builds his resentment to
the point of hate.

He who is rightly guided has hope
for he will have the ability to see good in all things and
to then act upon them.

He who is misguided will be despairing, unable to see
good in others.

He who is rightly guided has built trust through many
good actions.

He who is misguided has lost trust through many poor
actions.

He who is rightly guided values life works to its
preservation.

He who is misguided seeks death for many.

He who is rightly guided values the law, which is fair
judgement of action.

He who is misguided believes in social justice, the judgement of popularity and position in society.

He who is rightly guided and is responsible for his actions knows in the end, he will be judged.

He who is misguided believes he is not responsible for his actions and is ignorant of judgement.

He who is rightly guided, his many good actions have brought much gain by which many experience God, the joy of God.

He who has misguided actions lacks the goodness of God and has brought much loss due to the great deception of being just a self, and with it, all brought great sadness.

The self will one day die.

The rightly guided one is guided by the many ideas and values of God, for God is the ideal.

The one who is misguided is driven by many poor ideals and devalues of the Deceiver.

If there is anything a man should ask for, it is guidance.

The Philosopher had stated God was the ideal everything, that was ideal of someone could be assigned to God. The Deceiver was the un-ideal everything that was un-ideal of a person and could be projected into the Deceiver, in a dualistic value and devalued way of looking at the world.

To the Prophet, the Deceiver and God were more than just symbols. There was a realness to them that could only be called spiritual. He thought that it was somewhat foolish of the Philosopher to not take God more seriously, for if God willed it, one will walk up into the sky. The internal dialogue continued.

The Prophet said: Do not have any relationship with someone who does not enact the values of God within their lives, and watch how a person treats the weakest – that is their true character. Have no relationship with a person who preys upon the innocent and weak. Know the poor treatment they perform on the weak is the poor treatment you are likely to receive when you are weak.

The Philosopher said: Do not confuse lust for love, for both will make a man stumble. Lust be the want to express sexual desire, and it within itself is not love. Love is the feeling combined with good actions that says

"I want good for you". One without the other

is just good action or a feeling.

Good action be the only thing that separates love from

hate. For the feeling of love can make one feel good or

bad, and the feeling of hate can make one feel good or

bad. The only thing that truly separates love from hate

is actions. If one never displays any good actions, how

can another know if they are loved? The wish to express

one's lust can be an act of love or an act of hate. There

is no more dangerous concoction than the confusion of

love mixed with lust; it is the maddening desire.

The Prophet said: Do not be worried by your rebellious

nature for as there are many paths away from God,

there are many paths back to him. He who turns to the

Lord in good times is often better for it. One is meant to

be rebellious of that which is not of God, and the wicked

rebel against God.

Do not become wicked.

The Philosopher said: Know this, joy is greater than

happiness, for happiness is the absence of perceived

threat and joy is to experience a good gain, the

feeling of joy. Be aware of the ideas in one's head. One day you may unconsciously play them. Do not entertain thoughts of wickedness, they are like cards in the hand.

The Prophet said: Realise your mind is a temple that houses the Lord; he who houses the Lord, houses greatness. Do not forget your capacity for greatness; greatness is the opposite of evil. No man be great without God.

The Philosopher said: Do not underestimate your power for greatness to change yourself and the world incrementally for the better.

Dream of the great dream, realise one day when another stands on the earth, they live in your dream.

To become aware of the deterministic cycles to alter them into new cycles and the world will forever be changed.

Who is to know humanity's potential when it aims at greatness?"

The Philosopher said: Do not be blinded by hate and anger.

Anger is a reaction to perceived threat. It is the will to fight, and hate is the feeling combined with the actions which say, "I want no good for you".

Such a path is to destruction.

Do not be blinded by fear for it is another reaction to perceived threat. Also, it is to run, it is to be frozen on the spot, to tremble; it is the will to flee.

The Prophet was reminded late in the night of the great conversation he had with the Philosopher, who had explained feeling, how one should give a feeling a name and define it, then describe it in a way that can be positively integrated into one's life.

The Philosopher said to be territorial is the discontent one feels when something of theirs has been taken from them. Admiration is the appreciation of what someone else possesses while they possess it; envy is to covet what someone else possesses. So, know when something has been taken from you; know when to react; know when someone possesses something of their own; know to be happy for them; know not to be envious and covet what someone else possesses.

The Philosopher had also expressed a need for humanity to progress from such emotions as hatred, which is to want no good, to move onto more constructive feelings like the need to assert oneself or defence where one feels they need to defend themselves and even the need to flee. The feeling of assertion caused by poor actions one has done or one has received; one will perform actions within the law to cause a more positive outcome.

The feeling of defence where one feels threatened, and they need to defend themselves to use the law first and then to use physical force in defence if required. The feeling to flee where one is threatened to the point where they are not able to defend themselves and are caused to flee.

There are so many emotions that the Philosopher saw it as an unconquerable task to define them all, that we experience them primarily as an experience of internal feeling and often feel the need to act on them in an instinctive way. The defining of such emotions would allow reason to rule over feelings, rather than feelings to rule over reason.

He describes emotions as the waves of the sea, the person experiencing them as a wooden ship, that we are never fully in control of them; we are like the ship internally moved by them. As the ship's captain navigates the seas, so we should learn to navigate or correctly integrate our emotions.

That it is a flawed way to first look at emotions as a value or devalue because we experience them firstly, and then secondly, we can define and articulate them properly.

He said the one who obtains the highest highs often experiences the lowest lows, like a shipwreck at the bottom of the sea.

The Prophet had said "There is always hope; there is always God", and the Philosopher said, "Yes, and there is also modern medicine".

Late in the night there was identified one of the core values of a free nation, and it was tolerance. The

Philosopher defined the value as accepting within someone's freedom that every individual within their freedom will pursue different forms of good within their lives, and tolerance was to accept other people are entitled to that freedom. There was the paired devalue of intolerance, which was to not accept other people are entitled to different pursuits of good and to not tolerate it.

He had stated that the higher value of tolerance was not accepting wickedness or evil; it was merely accepting others' freedom. It was not the abandonment of one's own views, but to tolerate others, and he said you either believe in freedom or you will fall into extremism.

The Philosopher wished only to entertain the idea of morality in the mind. He knew it was so great that every individual should try to define their own, and in his own way, he was a guide to humanity.

The Prophet, like the Philosopher, wished to reintroduce the idea of God to humanity. He knew he was not sent as a final authority, and there would be many great ones after him, and in his own way, he had become a guide to humanity also.

The Prophet said there are two kinds of beauty. There is that which looks beautiful – the outward aesthetic; and beauty of action, where one's actions are so good, one can only describe them as beautiful. While the aesthetic beauty is desirable, beauty of action is how we change ourselves and the world for better.

Do not forget you are part of the great reality of God for God is real; he is the great reality of our time. You live and breathe God. If God so blesses you with children, bestow the values of God upon them; above all teach a child love. If you do, so long as your requests are reasonable, they will obey you in weakness and as you enter into old age.

God's love is the love that would lay down its life for another's good. It is the greatest of all values, for God so loved the world. Do not fall in love with the body for it is finite; you possess it for a time, the body dies, the soul does not. Man is forever looking for the link between the body and the soul. It is the imagination which resides in the temple of the mind, and many pass through this temple on their way to Paradise.

When man is stripped of his physicality, he is an idea. When he is forgotten, he is a soul.

As you look at your own reflection and see the body break down in decay, age, a slow torture in the throne room of the mind, as the god of self looks you in the face and tells you it is all meaningless, be grateful of one of God's many kindnesses – he gave you an immortal soul. You have a soul.

In unbearable pain and suffering is where you will find your God.

Know this, God is above every man; so it is that God's laws are above man's laws. They are of a higher standard; they are to be freely chosen for it benefits no-one that which is not done freely, God knows what is in the heart of man. Do not attempt to hold man to God's laws, only enforce when man wrongs man the laws of humanity. Paradise in the next life is not meant for all. Let them suffer or prosper in the reality that is God. Who is to know when someone will stumble upon God.

There is nothing more valuable than family and the love of God. God said it is not good for man to be alone. It is only by the grace of God that anyone was ever good, and it is only with God anyone is ever good.

Work to the limits of good that you can offer, where one's action are so wicked that they empower you to act. Then you shall prey on the wicked. Do not forget to use the law first, by which you will conquer, and secondly, physical might in defence.

Allow no principalities, groups or individuals to sway you into wrong. Stay on the straight narrow path for you will answer to God.

Do not be governed by desires but through reason and faith.

May your actions always point to God. May you walk with God all the days of your life into the hereafter.

If there is anything a man should ask God for, it is guidance.

The Prophet had walked the walk of a lifetime with God. His fate had been changed from that of a wicked man to the upright man with God. He knew he was unable to defeat the Deceiver, he could only leave words of guidance for humanity.

The words travelled through the air into the minds of the many people of the world. The seed, the idea of God, was implanted. The Prophet had travelled the world and had spoken of the many values of God and would continue to do so to his dying breath.

He had submitted to the Creator, which had brought peace, not only to the Prophet but to the many people of all different beliefs. This is how to tell if one submits to God – they will choose true peace. No true peace will ever be achieved without freedom; without it, there will be endless conflict.

He was near the end of his journey on earth. His body had become weak for we come into the world in a state of weakness, and we leave it in a state of weakness.

He cried out to God for aid, the Lord sent a fine lady, Kindness. She was young and beautiful even though she looked weak. There is great strength in kindness; in the end the world will be conquered by kindness.

Her lightest touch brought strength back into the Prophet's body. He walked his final steps upon the earth; he looked back and prophesied that humanity would prosper with God and suffer without him. The fine lady was the will of humanity renewed in God, the Prophet's anima, she goes by the names, Lady Love, Lady Wisdom and Lady Kindness.

Should humanity accept the reality of God, the fine lady will knock the harlot drunk on power, wealth and all manner of perversion off the beast of nations, into the waters below, to grab the heads of a dragon and hack them off with sword in hand, and there will begin humanity's era of long-lasting peace of reason and faith. The harlot is mankind's corrupted will. She goes by many names – Lady Hatred, Lady the Fool, Lady Wickedness – and her lightest touch will corrupt any man.

Humanity will be at war with itself between pleasure and pain to reason and faith. The harlot will wrestle the fine lady off the beast in corrupt times and vice versa in good times. The head of a dragon will forever wish to bite the heads off free nations.

As the fine lady is a part of the great reality of God, do not worship her, but God alone.

The fine lady had aided the Prophet. She then grew to be in scale with the grand size of the beast of nations, standing both on land and sea, she rode upon the back of the beast. She began to grab the heads of a dragon to cut them off one by one.

The image stays with the Prophet while his time drew short.

To stare into an endless blue.

All is God

7

THE ENDING

The world was forever changed.

Innocents, the intellectuals, the Prophet be martyrs'
food for flies in open fields, the great generals of the
world predetermine a different fate. They killed or
captured all the wicked. The wicked were tried under
the law by many good judges, who did not fail the Good
at arms; the world was filled with justice.

The environment was raised from a war zone to a
functional society. The rich businessman was able
to function under the safety of the law, which raised
many from poverty; the children did not starve. The
intellectuals educated the minds of the generation
instilling reason; the human morality before the law,

the governing power of the people, was changed in a generation.

The Prophet had spoken that of God and planted the idea of God in the many minds.

The Philosopher toiled over paper like a madman for his mind was filled with ideas for humanity. The world was a place of wonder, and he said, "I have defined it love, the greatest of all" in great excitement. The individual wrote a book, lived a joyful life filled with all the wonders of the intellectual world, and the world was changed. The man received many gifts. He lived a long life to see his grandchildren's children at the foot of his bed as he was about to die, and he was among those who died smiling.

The General stood above a sea of diverse flags, and he said, "I shall do what wicked men shall not". The world was conquered, and evil had no place to hide for the Good shall prey on the wicked.

His kind are immortalised.

There was a tactically minded individual who resided in an unknown location for he had predetermined the outcome in his mind to end all wars, and he said, "It will be as sure as the sun goes down and the moon rises with the tides".

He disappears to become likened to a chess piece in the game of life, in the mind of God.

The idea of conquering became synonymous with establishing free governments.

The Prophet was sitting on sandy beach for the man had found God in all things and he wished to prophesise peace over the world, but could not.

He said, "Until the world finds God, it will suffer needlessly".

He walked his final steps upon the earth, then onto the stairway leading into the night sky filled with luminous stars. The stairs were clear glass, a design that put mortal hands to shame, and allowed a picturesque view of the earth below. As the stairs spiralled around, it is not known what happened to the Prophet's body. Some say it fell to the earth, and the Prophet's soul wandered on into the night sky; others say it made it outside the earth's atmosphere and dissolved into space; the soul wandered into the heavens.

All that is known is the Lord was pleased with his faithful servant. The Prophet was and then he was not, for God had taken him.

God is all.

If there ever was a question humanity should answer, it is how to end evil in the world.

The End

ABOUT THE AUTHOR

Daniel Douglas is a novice intellectual, who lives in New South Wales, Australia, and works for a company that produces timber products.

He fills his leisure hours reading, watching intellectual conversations and daydreaming, and with his family. A religious and spiritual individual, he is influenced by Christian ideals.

Governance is the byproduct of countless hours of daydreaming, mainly focused on philosophy, war and peace. Daniel comes from a large family of eleven children and has his own family of four children, which he considers his greatest achievement.

The dream is to become one of the great thinkers of our time. The wish is to be considered a progressive thinker, one who believes in humanity evolving to a brighter future.

REFERENCES

The author used the Ten Commandments.

Ten Commandments list

You shall have no gods before me.

You shall not make any idols to worship.

You shall not take the Lord's name in vain.

Remember the Sabbath day and keep it holy.

Honour your father and your mother.

You shall not kill.

You shall not commit adultery.

You shall not steal.

You shall not bear false witness.

You shall not covet your neighbour's goods.

The author referred to these individuals as great ones, to allow for readers own interpretation of their character.

The Prophet Muhammad

The Qur'an 8.61

"And if they incline to peace, then you should incline to it; and put your trust in God."

Jesus's Christ

Mark 8.34-38

[36] For what shall it profit a man, if he shall gain the whole world, and lose his own soul?

Jesus simply quoted the words of Moses recorded in Deuteronomy 8:3 in reply, "It is written, 'Man shall not live on bread alone, but on every word that comes from the mouth of God'"

Matthew 4.4

John 14.6, Jesus proclaimed, "I am the way, and the truth, and the life. No-one comes to the Father except through me."

King Solomon

Proverbs 9.10-12New International Version (NIV)The fear of the Lord is the beginning of wisdom, and knowledge of the Holy One is understanding.

www.ingramcontent.com/pod-product-compliance
Lightning Source LLC
Chambersburg PA
CBHW050822090426
42738CB00020B/3451